BEFORE THE RAIN

Books by Luisita López Torregrosa

The Noise of Infinite Longing

Before the Rain

BEFORE
THE RAIN

A Memoir of Love and Revolution

LUISITA LÓPEZ TORREGROSA

HOUGHTON MIFFLIN HARCOURT
BOSTON   NEW YORK
2012

This is a work of nonfiction, a true account of my experiences as I remember them. However, I have changed some names, places, and identifying characteristics in order to protect the privacy of various individuals.

For information about permission to reproduce selections from this book, write to Permissions, Houghton Mifflin Harcourt Publishing Company, 215 Park Avenue South, New York, New York 10003.

www.hmhbooks.com

Library of Congress Cataloging-in-Publication Data
Torregrosa, Luisita López.
Before the rain : a memoir of love and revolution / Luisita López Torregrosa.
p. cm.
ISBN 978-0-547-66920-5
1. Torregrosa, Luisita López. 2. Journalists — United States — Biography.
3. Philippines — History — Revolution, 1986 — Personal narratives, American
I. Title.
PN4874.T6246A3 2012   070.92 — dc23
[B]   2011037314

Book design by Melissa Lotfy

Printed in the United States of America
DOC 10 9 8 7 6 5 4 3 2 1

Lines from "Vixen" from *The Vixen* by W. S. Merwin, copyright © 1995 by W. S. Merwin. Used by permission of Alfred A. Knopf, a division of Random House, Inc.

This book is for Kathy Robbins.

Comet of stillness princess of what is over
 high note held without trembling without voice without sound
aura of complete darkness keeper of the kept secrets
 of the destroyed stories the escaped dreams the sentences
never caught in words warden of where the river went . . .

— W. S. Merwin, "Vixen"

PART I

I

I N THE YEARS since that first letter came, postmarked New Delhi and written on pale lavender Claridges Hotel stationery, I have begun this story a hundred times, and each time I was afraid. We are entering winter now, much like the one, years ago, when I left my house and a dead relationship behind in the suburbs to stay at a friend's brick row house on a seedy street in the city, a bleak neighborhood of boarded-up ramshackle buildings, crack heads, and brown kids on roller skates. We called it Orchard House — a home for transient friends, broken hearts, and boozy evenings. Sooty, drafty, with creaking wooden floors and cigarette burns on the furniture, it was a place for great passions.

For a while that December, people came night and day, girls calling Tim on the phone, itinerant buddies bunking upstairs in rooms thick with dust and stale smoke. He had bought the house cheap from a couple who gave up on the block. Tim weeded the small patio out back, put in bricks, and planted tomatoes, basil, and rosemary, which, in wonder, I watched shoot up into city life. Gallery posters picked up in Italy, along with black-and-white blowups of grim scenes of poverty, were hung on the walls next to photos of dreamy girlfriends, all taken by his journalist colleagues and friends. Tim couldn't throw anything away; books were piled up on tables and desks, under his bed, and on bathroom shelves. He saved postcards, the sillier the better, and stuck them to the refrigerator, on mirrors, on the cupboards.

Any occasion was worth a party. For his big dinners, he walked several blocks to the farmer's market. There he stocked up on arugula, fennel, red lettuce, and shrimp or swordfish. He would cook up a huge pot of Cajun gumbo stew laced with so much Tabasco sauce, it burned the tongue. He was a dilettante cook, an improviser, who in a snap could create a dish out of nothing. He made it look simple, but he literally sweated out that stew, mopping his face and neck as he chopped onions and garlic, stirred the pot, tossed the salad, mixed drinks, and answered the buzzing doorbell. I used to watch him with envy on those nights, his curly hair matted, his shirt soaked, moving with ease from one guest to another, warming up the crowd, sometimes picking up his guitar and strumming a few chords. I marveled at how he spotted the overflowing ashtray, the empty wineglass, or the lone guest in a corner. I thought he would make a great wife.

Many evenings he was out late. There was nothing for me but the empty night with constant replays of my breakup of weeks earlier. Again and again, I remembered the winter chill in that rambling house in the suburbs as, over and over, I recalled the last words I said before I picked up my coat and slammed the back door, got into my car, and drove into the city to Tim's place. It was a cycle familiar to me: pursuit and ardor followed by domesticity, routine, sexual indifference, and the end. We unraveled slowly, going round in seemingly endless circles. By the time I walked out that evening in December 1985 with all the flourishes, tears, and drama the moment demanded, that relationship had been dying for a long time, and I had already fallen for someone else but could not admit it to anyone, not even to myself.

The routine of the workweek gave me only a semblance of ordinary life. I went through the motions, the mindless tasks, getting dressed in jeans, pinstriped shirt, V-neck sweater; picking up the papers thrown on the dining room floor, sorting out the sections, reading them front to back; no food, but cups of strong coffee. By ten o'clock I was bundled up in an old charcoal-gray overcoat and trundling down to work, passing a grubby bodega, a couple of old hardware stores, a twenty-four-hour takeout diner reeking of onions and burned grease, and homeless beggars wrapped in burlap rags, huddling for heat on steam grates. This part of town was a ruin, rusting away. I walked looking at the ground, the strap of my leather bag weighing my shoulder down, hands balled up in my coat pockets.

Thirty minutes it took me to arrive at the brass and glass doors of the newspaper, a 1920s gray and white tower with marble stairways, brass banisters, and the smell shared by newspapers the world around: ink, cigarette smoke, newsprint. Up on three, the newsroom was a sprawl of battered desks, scuffed floors, and fiberglass-enclosed cubbyholes. The Foreign Desk, where I was an editor, was jammed into the northeast corner of the newsroom. We sat elbow to elbow at a cluster of six desks set side by side in two rows, banging our chairs, overhearing each other's phone conversations, catching dribbles of gossip. I had the far-corner desk, where I could prop up my feet on a windowsill and get a glimmer of sky out a dingy window. Most of the time I was busy, reading and editing copy, empty coffee cups stacking up on my desk.

In those days the Foreign Desk had an aura. We had only six correspondents to cover the wars, revolutions, and coups of the mid-1980s: the carnage of civil war in Beirut, where the bombing of the U.S. Marines barracks ratcheted up round-the-clock mayhem; New Delhi, where Sikh guards assassinated Indira Gandhi, her bullet-ridden body bleeding out in her garden; Johannesburg, where the tragedy of racial hatred was played out in violence day after day.

Our reporters rode motorcycles and camels, let their hair grow long and marriages fail, drank heavily, and wandered off into the sub-Saharan deserts to tribal villages and remote refugee camps under siege. We kept a long list of national and metro reporters who wanted to grab the handful of overseas assignments, the plum jobs. They would come over to the desk and sidle up to the foreign editor, pitching their ideas, offering to go anywhere in the world, inflating their credentials (three languages, world travel, even a license in scuba diving).

We played up the romance of the job, tacking up on our bulletin board the postcards, souvenirs, and goofy snapshots of our correspondents fooling around, in baseball caps, khaki vests, sunglasses, arms manfully crossed on their chests as they lounged in swimming trunks against aqua blue seas and palm trees. Deskbound, wan under the newsroom's fluorescent lighting, we thought ourselves part of the action out there in the field, imagined ourselves inside the postcards as we sat eating

our bland lunches of Cobb salads and tuna sandwiches. It was
on the Foreign Desk that my longing for far places came out of
nowhere. I was terrified of flying and hadn't crossed any sea or
land in the air for years. But the stories out of Damascus, Eritrea
and Mombasa, Goa and Cairo, reminded me of my childhood in
hot countries, in the Caribbean, and traveling from Puerto Rico
to Havana to Mexico City, where my father studied medicine.
They reminded me too of my mother, slowly turning the pages
of a copy of the *National Geographic*, pointing at the places that
one day she would visit.

Our days on the desk were punctuated by crises and disasters, occasional bombings. We straggled into the quiet mornings, logged on to and scrolled through the wires, looking out
for Associated Press bulletins from godforsaken places such as
Bhopal, a city in central India where a Union Carbide pesticide
plant leaked clouds of toxic gas and chemicals and thousands
died. The desk went into high gear immediately. In a flash the
desk clerk had tracked down our man in New Delhi and figured
out how quickly he could travel the four hundred and sixty-four
miles south to Bhopal. The question of how he would file his
copy from a devastated area—by telephone or telex—in time
to meet the newspaper's deadline was quickly settled. With bad
phone connections and downed lines, it was never easy to report
out of India. Bhopal took days.

Aside from the crises, the days on the desk were pretty much
set. Arriving in midmorning wearing dusty biker boots and a
helmet, the foreign editor looked through the messages on his
cluttered desk, scrolled through the incoming news, and studied
the world map pinned above his desk, playing with the pushpins,

moving them from one place to another, marshaling his troops. Dave had a knack for sniffing out the next big story, as well as a soft hand with weary correspondents who were fighting malaria or censorship, dangerous travel or complaining wives. Sizing up the day, how the stories were developing, who was writing what, Dave parceled out editing assignments to the four or five editors working. We were not shy about stepping on each other's turf. I had Latin America and wanted to add South Asia. Somebody else had Moscow, and someone Africa, and so on, but there were no set boundaries. No one truly owned anything. Tensions and jealousies ran under the surface, and the jostling for territory was quite apparent when an editor tried to dominate a big story or had a favorite writer. Unlike some of the other editors who had been on the desk for years, I hadn't met any of the correspondents and hardly knew Dave.

I would come in to work early, trying to get ahead of everyone else, check the wires and overnight messages. Legs tucked under me, shoulders hunched, rocking back and forth, I trolled the files and kept an ear out to pick up threads of conversations going on around me. I went for days on coffee and Diet Coke. Around six o'clock someone on the desk would sing out, "Miller time!" and we would sign off for the day and cross the street to Looney's. In those days every newspaper had its bar, usually a dive, and Looney's was our dive. Picture the squeaky screen door, neon beer signs, gummy linoleum floors, the jukebox and scuffed pool table out back. I huddled up in a booth, dropped a quarter into the slot, and called out for longnecks. I kept my empties lined up on the table, peeling off the labels and talking shop with other editors and a reporter or two. We lingered past dinnertime and then, one by one, closed out the tab and made our way out.

She came out of nowhere, bookish and terribly proper in her tortoiseshell-frame glasses, as if she had just left Miss Chapin's. They called her Blake. Genderless and a touch literary, her name drew attention, set her apart.

On the day we first met, a Sunday in early 1985, ten months before my breakup, she was on duty on the City Desk and assigned to fill in details in a wire story I was handling about a group of Americans detained in Honduras. I had never read her articles, which appeared in a suburban edition, and had never seen her before.

"She's very sharp," the city editor assured me, but I was skeptical. She was sitting a few desks away, her eyes fixed on the computer screen. She turned her face up to me slowly when I approached, as if surprised that someone had dared to stir the air around her. I introduced myself, made a couple of suggestions, and offered to help her with the Honduran telephone operators and the Tegucigalpa bureaucrats. She listened politely, and then, in a tone that showed both deference and confidence, she let me know that she could speak Spanish and had already made the phone calls.

I was taken aback and stood there awkwardly, managing a muttered compliment. An hour or so later, she sent her story to my computer terminal; I gave it a quick read and waved at her to come over to my desk. She pulled up a chair next to mine, stretched her legs up on the desk, and, without saying anything, watched me read it. She was spare, with wavy reddish hair fluffed and brushed back behind her ears. She was wearing tiny gold earrings, loose cotton pants, a shirt with the sleeves rolled up. Her head leaned only inches away from mine. She spoke only to answer my questions and to make a point here and there, and she didn't resist, like so many of our reporters did, when I touched up a line or two.

"There, now we have a real news story," I heard myself say a bit dismissively when I was done editing, pretending detachment but actually taken by her poise, a guarded manner that permitted no intrusion. She had such an austere exterior, a patrician face, long-jawed, pale, and angular. In her cardigan sweater and woolen vest, she reminded me of the girls I had known in prep school, the tennis players and swimmers who spent summers sailing or touring France. She had that patina — expensive schools, flute lessons, maids in uniform, rigid discipline.

She typed in her byline, E. Blake Whitney — Elizabeth Blake Whitney. She pushed back her chair, jumped up, and thanked me with a fast handshake, then walked away, head high, hands in pockets, her stride long and quick.

I didn't see her again for months.

Nobody in the newsroom knew much about her. She didn't burst on the scene, parading her résumé and her private life. She didn't come to the parties, to the big announcements, the periodic celebrations for one award or another. But she had a canny charm, a honed sense for luring the powerful, dropping by the managing editor's office from time to time, his freckled face brightening at the sight of her. He remembered that page of her unfinished novel she had slipped in among her newspaper clippings. It was the main reason he hired her, taken in not only by her writing but by the gall she showed, sending him a piece of fiction.

It was rare to find, he said, among the piles of applications he sorted through every day, a talent like hers. She could turn a phrase, he said, an extravagant compliment coming from him. A short essay she did that spring for the paper's Sunday magazine about living in the suburbs had the rhythm of a tone poem, he said, and she could get into people's heads. "You should read her interviews. You could put them right into the paper just as they are." The newspaper had platoons of reporters knocking on doors and poring over documents, doing the paper's famous investigations, but she made it a point to work alone, outside the bustle of the newsroom, and she did not whine for attention; she did not overplay her hand. On the desks she worked—Suburban, National, Metro—they said she was the ideal reporter: resilient, self-contained, a good soldier.

On the few occasions when she came to the main office in the city from her rounds in the suburbs, I watched her from a wary distance, annoyed that her presence—a walk through the newsroom, a passing smile, a quick wave—could wreck my concentration. I would catch her gazing at me, her eyes drifting in my direction while her body was turned to someone else, and then she would swiftly turn her back on me and I would return to my work, fidgeting at my desk, pretending to ignore her.

One weekend in July, a few months after we had first met, on a day I was busy reading a piece that she and another metro reporter had written for the front page, she came over to the desk and stood leaning against a radiator not far from me. Another reporter was seated near me, his legs dangling off my desk, making himself at home, asking how he could get a foreign assignment. He wanted to put his name on that list. Leaning against a radiator, she listened to him, silently amused.

Quietly, she asked me, "So how does one get on the list?" I was surprised that she would bring up the question directly. "You just tell me," I said, turning my full attention to her. She nodded, her eyes fixed on my face, and it crossed my mind that she might be playing me to get what she wanted.

The next day I stopped by the managing editor's office and mentioned her name for a spot coming open, a six-week assignment in Nicaragua, the new killing field of Central America where the revolutionary Sandinistas were at war with the Contra rebels financed by the Central Intelligence Agency. He stared at me, startled, his reading glasses pushed up on his forehead, crinkles around his icy Nordic eyes. "She won't go," he said with a flick of his wrist, dismissing the thought. "She just got married and bought a house, and she's not going to leave it for two months."

But the idea piqued his interest. He had on his sly grin, usually inscrutable, but I had known him long enough and sometimes could read his poker face. "Bet she'll go," I said, taunting him, poking a finger in his arm and then leaving his office.

Several weeks later he offered her the Nicaragua assignment. It took her two seconds to take it.

I rushed to invite her out to dinner, something I did with many of the reporters coming onboard. Walking up the street by the paper, where a few old warehouses and rundown buildings had been turned into bistros and lofts, we fumbled to fill the awkward gaps in our conversation. She was diffident, careful with me, and kept a foot of distance between us, her face look-ing down or straight ahead. I, trying to impress her, to make my mark early, barraged her with questions, drawing her out, and making sweeping statements about the desk, about the mis-sion. We found a table by the bar, ordered wine, and looked over the menus for a long time. She took a cigarette from my pack, struck a match with the edge of a fingernail, and flipped it into the ashtray, her hand shaking slightly. Her eyeglasses reflected the restaurant lights and partly concealed her deep-set aquama-rine eyes, but I noticed that her gaze didn't waver. She had me pinned.

We drank one glass, then another. After a while, after the half-truths strangers tell each other about their lives—she never mentioned her private life and I didn't ask—she leaned forward and pushed up her chair, seeming more at ease. Sounding pomp-ous even to myself, I told her that foreign reporting was a call-ing, strenuous, solitary, and obsessive. Embellishing as I spoke, I said that few people had a natural knack for it, and that I guessed she might have it. I was courting her with words, flattering her and exaggerating my importance at the same time. She seemed drawn in right away and came up with stories she would do in Nicaragua, recalling her trips to Mexico, the purple of the sier-ras, the Yucatán ruins, the mood of the people, the language.

She had read *The Conquest of the Incas,* and Latin American poets and novelists, and one year after college when she was living in Europe she taught herself Spanish after visiting the Basque region—she had fallen for the barren broodiness of the place, and the food!

It didn't seem to make a difference to her that Nicaragua was a tinderbox, that villages were carpet-bombed day and night and the city of Managua was a blazing hole—or, more likely, that is why she sought the assignment. She liked the romance of it, the intensity of life lived so closely to death.

Nicaragua didn't happen. The paper went on strike for almost two months, and she stayed away from the office. But when we went back to work in the fall, she was playful, inquiring about the desk, prodding me about her prospects and passing along compliments she had heard about me—ingratiating herself with flattering comments of the kind I had heard from other reporters politicking to land a foreign bureau. But I was taken in anyway.

After the strike that fall, she was settling back in to her beat and, on days off, painting her house and planting a garden. Around that time, Nick, our correspondent in New Delhi, announced that he was leaving the newspaper at the end of that year, in December 1985. He had a good offer somewhere else. Half a dozen reporters immediately lined up for Nick's job, the South Asia bureau. To everyone's surprise, the editors offered it to her—they were giving her all of Asia. She would have to leave for India within two months, in January 1986, just after Christmas. "India's perfect for you," I said, a bit overexcited. She had spent all day talking to the brass and was now worn out, slouching in a chair at the Foreign Desk and looking quite pained. "Don't push me," she warned. "I don't think I can do it."

For weeks she agonized. This was not Nicaragua, a two-stop, four-hour flight from home, a quick turnaround. Asia was a universe away. There was her husband, her parents, her new house.

Finally, alone, sitting in a pew at a church a few blocks from the newspaper, she decided to go.

All this—her phone calls, her notes, her turmoil—drew me in day by day and kept my mind off the drastic changes in my own life, the end of a longtime relationship, the gloom of that house I had come to hate in the suburbs, and finally my move to the city.

In the weeks before her departure for New Delhi, she would send elliptical messages, unsigned, undated, disrupting my day. Sometimes the whole damned deck gets reshuffled all at once, she said, making fun of herself and her habit of planning everything. Exhilarated but afraid, she was riding an emotional seesaw. It was rare for her to acknowledge such things to someone else. "It's an irony that I somehow find you the easiest and most difficult person to talk to," she said, annoyed.

Some days she sat only feet from me, among the other editors on the Foreign Desk, and ignored my presence. She was going through the basics on the desk, learning the routine, deadlines, how to file stories from abroad. I noticed that some of the desk editors seemed a bit wary of her intensity and cool reserve, a manner they took for cold-blooded and cocky. While talking to them, she averted her eyes from me, but before leaving the desk she would turn and brush my shoulder with the tips of her fingers on the way out.

One evening later that winter, after Christmas and New Year's, on the first Monday in January 1986, Tim made a small, intimate dinner for three—grilled swordfish, good wine, candles, flowers in a bud vase—and he invited her. He invited her for me. I had been persistent, pressing him, telling him about her. "Yes, she hangs the moon," Tim agreed. "Yes, she's beautiful. Yes, she's brilliant . . . but you're crazy." He wasn't smiling, saying that. "You know she's married. It's no good."

I felt the burn. He had me there. I was crazy.

But I didn't back down.

You're wrong, I told him, you'll see.

She would pass me notes and saunter over to my desk, smelling of Chanel No. 19, and toss me a candy bar or a new tape of the Talking Heads she particularly liked. When she thought I wasn't looking, she glanced out of the corner of her eye at me and pulled on my sweater. "You look good," she said as she kept walking. Those mornings when I came in early to check the wires, I looked for her car in the parking lot and sensed her presence across the newsroom: the slope of her shoulders, the trailing scarf she threw around her long neck, her flowing red hair.

She came to Tim's that night in blue jeans and laced-up hiking boots, holding out a warm loaf of cranberry bread she had baked. Tim was in the kitchen, broiling the swordfish steaks, humming to himself, a dirty apron tied around his waist, and I was fluttering nervously, bringing her a drink, handing her a cigarette, jumping up to put on the music she wanted. There was nothing stiff about her as she shucked off her field coat and scarf and gloves, feeling free from the eyes in the office. Here at Orchard House, among the knickknacks and battered furniture, she seemed able to breathe and relax. "It's like the third world here," she said, looking around. "Not like my mother's house, you know, with all the white furniture."

She had Scotch. I had wine. Tim was effusive, at his most charming, making her laugh, her arms resting on the table, her hands gesturing, and her head thrown back. We were high halfway through dinner, clinking glasses, toasting Tim, who was going to Manila on temporary assignment, and toasting her, too, and her new job in Asia. They would work together in the Philippines but he would get there before her. She needed more time to plan a three-year assignment and had to first go to New Delhi to the furnished flat Nick had rented, which doubled as the paper's bureau. Eventually she would get to Manila. They cheered each other like old colleagues, but I sensed an edge to their banter, a hint of rivalry.

Attentive to Tim, she sat close to me, held cupped hand to chin, her index finger poised over her mouth, a typical pose. With Tim filling our glasses and playing the Coltrane blues on his record player, we told each other stories — my climb from small-town newspapers in the South; her choice of a college far from her roots in the East, where she cloistered herself, studying night and day, graduating cum laude and getting a Phi Beta Kappa key; Tim's auspicious beginning as a cub reporter chasing stories in Manhattan for a wire service, and his jazzy days as a radio DJ in college. After the coffee and the cognac, Tim cleared the dishes and stacked them on the counter for me to wash later, and went out, leaving us alone. I didn't dare move from the table and kept talking and filling her glass and got drunk.

Long past midnight, she had to go, and we walked out to her car and sat on a neighbor's stoop. It was freezing that night, with slippery ice on the sidewalk, and ice on the stone stoop. We were worn out, drained, and the street was silent, the sky blue-black, starless. I touched her hand, and she turned her eyes away from me and began to cry. "I'm afraid I'll use you, and hurt you," she said, pulling her hand away. I was knocked back, surprised at the implied threat. You could never hurt me, I lied. But feeling slapped back, I ran down the street, hoping she would follow. She didn't. When I got back to the house, she was gone.

A few days later Tim left for Manila to cover the presidential campaign of Ferdinand Marcos and Corazon Aquino, which had the world riveted. So many foreign journalists had descended on Manila that the campaign took on the aspect of an epic, a crusade of good against evil. Marcos had ruled the Philippines with an iron hand and stolen millions of dollars that he had stashed away in Swiss banks. He was a sick old man, riddled with lupus, but he still wielded power, and had the military behind him. On the other side was a political amateur, Cory Aquino, diffident, frail, soft-spoken, the widow of the nation's leading opposition leader, Benigno S. Aquino Jr., assassinated three years earlier, in 1983, in what everyone believed was a Marcos plot. Cory had students behind her, along with the middle class and the elite, and an anxious business sector. She had something invaluable then. She had a name revered in her country, synonymous with democracy and freedom. No one that January in 1986 expected Cory to win as the months-long campaign headed to a close on Election Day, February 7. Marcos controlled the election machinery, bought votes wholesale — and violence was rampant, hundreds killed in the provinces, even in Manila in broad daylight.

Tim and I had scanned travel guides, books on Philippine politics and history, articles on Marcos's hidden wealth and his twenty-year regime, and stayed up nights discussing the stories he would file, putting together a plan. Brilliant and excitable, prone to lyrical hyperbole, Tim glamorized the place, dreaming of romance and meeting up with warlords. In his white jeans and shiny black boots, he hugged me goodbye out on the sidewalk, and he was grinning wildly, a boy off on an adventure.

Suddenly I was alone in his house, its creaking stairs and dirty kitchen, and the night noises of frayed window blinds flapping in the wind and empty whiskey bottles hurled in the backyard. The mornings were dreary. With Tim gone, there were no heavy footfalls awakening me, there was no jazz playing at seven-thirty on the old radio in the bathroom, no crumpled newspapers on the breakfast table, no fresh coffee waiting.

Every day I hurried to the office, looking for her. Halfway through the day, breaking away from the desk, I would meet her in the cafeteria. We didn't bring up the warning she had given me that night at Tim's, and she didn't stay away from me. One afternoon we were sitting at a table by the window in the cafeteria, barely touching the stale coffee, talking easily and looking out at the recently fallen snow piled on the sidewalks, when suddenly she interrupted me. "Why don't you write?" she said. "The way you talk, you should be a writer. That's who you are . . . You just don't know it yet." I was stunned. I stammered, coughing the cough that came when I was nervous. "I don't say this lightly," she said. "I've never told anyone this: that they should write. Few people really can, and it's horribly hard. But you are a writer. I know that much about you." I used to write, I told her, when I was much younger, in college, years ago, but now I don't even have a typewriter.

The next time she came to Orchard, on a Saturday after work, she brought an old Smith Corona she had picked up in a junk store and had rebuilt with new bolts and a new black ribbon. With a triumphant smile, enjoying the look of surprise on my face, she hauled it in and set it on the dining table, bulky black metal with clanking keys. She had rolled a sheet of paper on it and typed a brief note: "Some really very fine writing lurks inside this old machine," I remember it said. "I hope you find it where, too often, I did not."

That night we had dinner at a restaurant near the river, the sort of place she would never have chosen—too expensive, pretentious, with long-haired male waiters in slick black uniforms. The white-clothed tables were brightened with fresh-cut freesias set in miniature porcelain vases. We ordered a bottle of Cabernet Sauvignon and felt celebratory, but I had a sense of danger, too, of daring too much. I brought up her husband and her mood soured immediately. I could feel her closing up, going cold. With some hesitation, she said that he already knew about me. So much was at stake, she said—her family, the life she had constructed, solid, secure. She had hardly slept for weeks. It's not easy, she pleaded. After dinner we drove to Orchard. She stretched out on the living room rug, her back leaning against the coffee table. I put on Brahms and sat cross-legged across from her, smoking a cigarette. We didn't talk for a long time and then she said under her breath that she hadn't listened to Brahms in ten years. She seemed pained, her eyes welling up, a tear on her cheek. I moved toward her. She didn't say a word.

We had a short time. Eight days. She was leaving at the end of

the month for India to get settled in the apartment Nick had recently left. From there she was going to join Tim in Manila, where
she would stay for an indefinite amount of time. In those last
days together, thinking ourselves so secretive, we left our tracks
everywhere. Drinking beer after work at Looney's, sprawled in
a booth, with people all around us but thinking ourselves alone.
Meeting on the back stairs of the paper to go shopping for a tape
deck she wanted to take to New Delhi. She loved to drive by the
airport at night, slowing down to watch the planes take off and
land, and then speeding down the expressway, the moon roof of
her midnight blue Volkswagen wide open to the winter wind,
Patti LaBelle at full volume, her hand clutching mine.

Those moments with each other when nothing else mattered
and we seemed to move and think in unison didn't last long. She
was uncertain about what was happening between us, stressed
about her work, anxious about living in a foreign place so far
from home. I barreled through doubts, and my persistence often
pushed her away. She talked time and again about the long view,
the future beyond this moment. On the day she left, I had waited
for her at home. She rang the bell and wouldn't look straight
at me when she crossed into the living room, her trench coat
belted and a scarf knotted at her throat. She looked pale, with
deep circles under her eyes, hollow sockets, her jaws clenched.

"I'll see you in Manila," I promised, sitting her down by me
on the couch. "I'll see you in Manila," I repeated as if saying it
twice made it true. "It is destiny," I said, knowing she laughed
at that sort of talk. But she didn't laugh, just looked down and
bit her lower lip. She didn't believe me. The unsettling feeling

that kept her up at night would disappear once she was gone, she said. It was fleeting, an abstraction. "I'll just be happy to know you are out there on the planet," she said, something she would repeat over the years. She rose to go, her arms abruptly around me, and just as suddenly she left. I watched her walk slowly toward her car, never looking back.

The letter on pale lavender stationery arrived a week later. I opened it carefully.

She was seated in her flat in New Delhi, she said, surrounded by newspaper clips detailing a crisis going on in the Punjab and feeling guilty because she couldn't concentrate. She was dazzled by the city and how comfortable it seemed to her, as if it had been her destiny — something I would appreciate — as if she was meant to be there.

The trip had been difficult, she said, and I guessed, reading between the lines, that she had decided to end her marriage.

I could envision her there, with the myna birds and the black bats that hung off tall, gnarled trees, the parrots and the rare birds she could not identify. I pictured her in her stucco apartment, seated barefooted on her dhurrie, drinking Kingfisher beer under the ceiling fan. She had bought a pair of Indian chairs made of handwoven straw and carved wood, with low round legs four inches off the ground. She had bartered for them at a roadside market a few days after she arrived in New Delhi, and she had bartered too for a carving of the head of a lion and for a battered old steamer trunk of unknown origin with heavy, rusted iron handles and weathered wood stained a coral green. These were her furnishings, along with the handmade desk with the bottle-green leather top that someday would be mine.

She would go running early in the morning down the tree-shaded boulevards where tiny women dressed in cotton saris bent over hand brooms, sweeping the red dust that coats the city. The heat would rise slowly, the white heat that came with dawn, bleaching the exterior of buildings, the inside walls, even the curtains. By noon it blanked everything out, choking all breath. Tropical heat descends like a vast dampness blown in by trade winds, but the heat of India turns the sky white. No one goes out, nothing stirs. The cows sleep in the shade of drooping trees, the soldiers who guard the parks nap bare-chested on stretchers under canvas tents, their shirts hung out on lines to dry. The birds vanish into the trees, and sidewalk vendors crouch under cardboard boxes, their heads draped in rags.

She could walk through those streets without meeting a friendly face, and in the dim stores the merchandise—thick cotton sheets and silken fabrics, sandpapery toilet tissue and scented soap—lay in plastic covers filmed with dust. In bookshops the paperbacks ran to Marx and Engels, musty with age, their corners curled. There was an earthen hue to the city: colonial grays against the stark desert red of government mausoleums gave New Delhi an austerity far removed from the steel and glass and flashing neon of the modern world. Deeper into the city, Old Delhi reeked of death. Filthy alleys, foul food markets, vegetables and spoiled meat and chickens spread out in the muck. Flies crawled over everything, and children with runny noses and muddy hands, moaning and whining, pulled at your clothes, kissing your feet. Multitudes spilling out from crumbling buildings, from stores, from buses, from brothels and mosques, taking up every centimeter of city space, all yelling, gesticulating, chattering and chanting in one monumental human chorus. There were no brilliant colors, only a pastel wash over all of it against a soil the shade of dried blood.

Orchard House was freezing. The old furnace didn't work. The man came to repair it, but it was still cold, the wind sifting through the window cracks. At night the streets turned dead quiet aside from neighbors parking their cars and slamming doors, and the muffled footsteps of passersby. I huddled inside, keeping myself warm with wine and music and clacking at the old typewriter she had given me. How I loved that sound! I had built a cocoon, a safe house for my secrets, telling myself stories, fantasies. At night I wrote her letters on yellow copy paper, typing until dawn. I drank white wine and ate cold pasta. I mused over her letters and stashed them away, one by one, in chronological order, and bound them in rubber bands.

By this time she had left New Delhi and had flown to Manila to cover the election. Manila was a newsreel I played over and over in my mind. I could see her there too, a head taller than anyone else, in her ponytail, khakis, and tennis shoes, always striding, always in a hurry, a ruthlessly ambitious young foreign correspondent. She had believed that leaving America would mean leaving behind the feeling that unnerved her—her attraction to me, her fear of me. But instead we became at that distance an overwhelming presence to each other, intimate and constant, in letters and phone calls. I made her a tape of crescendos and

adagios, and she mixed a cassette piecing together Van Morri-
son, Aretha Franklin, Phil Collins, Sting. She called it Manila
Blues.

I played it until it was etched in my mind.

I can feel it coming in the air tonight, oh, Lord . . .

Mornings I arrived at work to find messages in my computer—a two-liner from her, often lighthearted, but at times
clipped, all business: thousands of people at an Aquino rally,
snarled traffic, guards with M16s on rooftops. Every day we
talked on the telephone, at the office in the morning and at home
in the evening, looping conversations and long silences that
never ended anywhere and left us dazed.

She dashed off postcards and scribbled notes on the run and
wrote long letters when she had a rare day off and could let go
under the billowing clouds of the tropics, drinking double margaritas at a poolside table at the Manila Hotel. She drew pictures
of the kidney-shaped swimming pool with its sunken thatched-
roof bar. She sketched the tourists and reported on the comings-
and-goings of the hotel staff, who annoyed her, whistling at her.
She lingered all afternoon in the shade of the banyan trees by the
pool and wondered if she would ever belong there.

She always wrote with a fountain pen, in blue-black or brown
ink. She was the only person I knew who kept bottles of ink
and carried them with her. She wrote her letters to me in long-
hand, in a tight, slashing twist, the ending of words thrown back,
or trailing off, as if she wanted to take it all back, and closing
abruptly, without a period, with that illegible signature—Elizabeth.

2

FROM AFAR, IN AMERICA, the Philippines has always evoked Hollywood images of the Pacific battles of World War II, the death march at Bataan, the bunker island of Corregidor, the charred airfields of Luzon. General MacArthur, corn pipe in mouth, cinematic in sunglasses, wading ashore on Leyte. War stories overheard in bars, freeze-frames of history. There has been, always, a celluloid quality to the country, a staged extravagance.

So it was in February 1986, when Manila once again became a front-page story, a daily feature on the evening news. Americans were mesmerized again by the place, fascinated by a melodrama unfolding before our eyes: the fall of Marcos.

Killings in the provinces, lost ballot boxes, chaos on Election Day, rumors of coups, and, finally, the revolution. Manila was larger than life, with more intrigue and conspiracies than the best soap opera — and far more exotic. It was at last one of those countries where we could tell villain and hero apart, where the lines were absolute: Cory Aquino, a tiny bespectacled woman, goes up against the twenty-year tyranny of the hated Ferdinand

Marcos, and a cast of millions of sweet little people smile and weep for the cameras.

Before that year I had hardly given the country a thought, but that winter the Philippines felt intimately familiar, recalling long-buried memories of my childhood in the Caribbean — sun-baked gardens, panoramic mountains and palm trees, tropical translucent sea, and the poor. An archipelago of seventy-one hundred islands stretching from the Tropic of Capricorn in the north to the equator in the south, lying almost parallel to the West Indies, the Philippines seemed oddly out of place: What was an old Spanish colony with ancient cathedrals and Spanish names doing out there, thirteen thousand miles away, in the South China Sea, lost in the tropics of Asia?

After work I kept the television on in my bedroom for the overnight news from Manila, where it was already the next day. There was Cory dressed in yellow, the color of her campaign, wraithlike, kneeling at an altar. Here was Ferdinand Marcos stooping and limping, and Imelda, a boulder behind him, shouting to the heavens, *"Marcos pa rin!"* ("Marcos forever!"). On the other side, the mammoth crowds in yellow T-shirts, hundreds of thousands of Cory's people rising across Manila in a swell of anti-Marcos chants, *"Tama na! Tama na!"* ("Enough! Enough!"). I absorbed every detail, the backdrops, the skyline, the faces, the names of streets, the hotel façades, until I had mapped out the city in my head. Manila raw. The open sewers. The primitive art. Too many centuries of too much heat and too many boots trampling its soil.

Just as I was falling asleep, the phone would ring, shrieking

in my ear. Jolted fully awake, I waited for the seashell-roar of
the overseas line to clear. And then the click, Elizabeth's voice.
It could be anything—a cheery good-night call, or questions:
Should she cover that press conference or go to the slums and
talk to "real" people; should she change hotel rooms again; were
her stories making any sense; was I writing? Or it could be a
night of insomnia, a fight on the phone with her husband, who
had stayed behind and was not agreeing to a divorce and wanted
to go see her in Manila.

What did you say? I asked, alarmed.

I told him not to come, she said after a pause, but he's coming
anyway.

I couldn't sleep after that.

Days later, her voice was a reed, thin and tired, on the morning she called me after she had nearly fainted inside a crowded
cathedral where Cory Aquino was speaking. And it was frantic
on the afternoon when the military revolt against Marcos started
in Manila and Elizabeth found herself hundreds of miles from
the action, in the central island of Cebu, where she had gone for
a rally with Cory and was left stranded, scrambling to get on a
plane to take her back to the capital. It didn't help her anxious
mood that Cory had vanished and was said to be hiding somewhere.

Occasionally, less often, it was Tim on the line. Brisk, hoarse
from smoking Dunhills, bursting with news, gossip, reports on
Elizabeth, except he usually called her "Whitney, Whit!" Once
again she had trounced him on the tennis court, he said, and
got a sprained toe running on the court. Tim loved women, all

women, and Elizabeth Blake Whitney was high up there on his list. But they had separate assignments. He was following the Marcos campaign and she was covering Cory, and there was friction under the camaraderie, a friendly but tenacious rivalry for front-page play and at times my attention. With his easy patter and affectionate manner, he was a fair-minded competitor, praising Elizabeth, saying she had a magic wand, but he had a ferocious drive and bristled when anyone beat him on a story. Hard on himself, harder than we on the desk could ever be, he took it all out on himself, not eating, not sleeping, his nerves on edge.

One day he called up breathless, shaken. He had had a narrow escape at a Marcos rally where shooting had broken out. A reporter Tim knew was grazed by a bullet while she stood close to him, and he could still smell the blood. Another time his wallet was snatched out of his knapsack and his press credentials ripped off, and there were innumerable times when his days were spent outrunning the flying stones of the Marcos crowds. But his main concern always was this: Were his stories getting play, was he beating the competition, was he missing anything? I would reassure him on the phone, but he knew me too well; he knew Elizabeth took up most of my time, and no apologies from me could make up for that. I could see him rifling through the canvas bag I had given him, ballpoint pens spilling all over the room, coins falling out of his pocket, rushing around, stoop-shouldered, shaggy-haired, children hanging by his shirttails. All this was far more real to me than my days at work, the rattling furnace, the newsroom gossip, linguini dinners at trendy trattorias, and incessant talk of real estate.

Twice, three times a week Elizabeth's phone calls or letters came. Sometimes just single sheets, sometimes a batch arriving on the same day, stiff and musty, like the smell of old books, of things that have traveled an immense distance. She recounted her days, often mundane, occasionally scary, and sometimes she imagined me there with her, close by. So much was left unsaid, but quarrels could break out suddenly over the phone. She used to say, with a bit of sarcasm, that I was in the constant and brutal pursuit of the truth, and she balked at that. She wanted to calibrate things, calibrated her words, her emotions. I calibrated nothing. She asked me to be patient, but I was never patient, and finally, worn down, with a glacial edge in her voice, she would cut me off with a curt "OK, bye" and hang up the phone. Stumped and frustrated, I would sit in Tim's armchair, kicking myself in the half-lit gloom.

One day not long after we had talked for hours and nothing, it seemed, was left to be said, a letter came, written with the abandon she urged in me but rarely allowed herself. I read it a dozen times. She had always pictured herself a loner, going about life on her own, but now she wanted to share everything. I could only guess what it had taken out of her to express so much emotion so directly, breaking down barriers she had put up. I knew then I would go to Manila.

The revolution, which had seemed spontaneous, an improvisation, lasted just seventy-two hours. The truth of the events has long ceased to matter, a mythical story now after the years and the legends have consumed it, transformed it. They called it the People Power Revolution, bloodless and full of song and prayer:

the day the nuns stopped the tanks and plaster statues of the Virgin were carried through streets blackened by smoke from burning tires. The day, February 25, 1986, when Cory Aquino, wearing yellow lace, was sworn in as the eleventh president of the Philippines, and Marcos, with his puffy face and bandaged hands, was airlifted with Imelda from the presidential palace by American helicopters and flown to Clark Air Base and on from there to exile and death, in 1989, in Hawaii.

Around the newsroom we had kept score, cheerleaders on the sidelines. Standing on desks, on chairs, clustered around the TV set up on a wall, we watched each episode that day until the final scenes of euphoric Filipinos mashing portraits of Marcos, climbing over the gates of Malacañang in a rampage, looting Imelda's rooms, trashing everything in sight. The stars of the American TV networks, blow-dried and suited for their Manila Hotel stand-ups with proper furrowed brows and smug attitude, savored this triumph. It was no small victory for the foreign press, which had hounded Marcos for years and had descended on Manila by the hundreds that February, and could now pick at the bones.

In all the commotion, in the insane rush I had lived on for weeks, I wasn't braced for the inevitable: the deflation that comes after a big story is over. There are no credits at the end, no lights coming on. What occurs is a kind of drawdown, a disengagement from battle. We had our postmortems at the desk and our rounds at Looney's, and pats on the head from up high, gushy notes from the managing editor I would stick on my fridge. But the strain began to come out in the open. Jealousies, sniping, gossip, telegraphic glances, lowered eyes. I had trampled on other editors, grabbing the story for myself. I had blurred the lines, had become too involved with the story and the reporters, especially with Elizabeth. I had lost control and had also lost ten pounds, bitten my nails to the quick, and more than once made a fool of myself when the news editor demanded a rewrite of Elizabeth's stories and I disagreed. It's time to let go of the story, Dave told me one night, kindly drawling it out, but with a knowing glance.

For Tim, the assignment was over, and he was dejected. On the phone he sounded exhausted, edgy, curt, totally unlike his usual self. He began to dump on his own work and complain about the desk. Had I failed him, I wondered silently, had I been too preoccupied with Elizabeth? He didn't say, but I had not paid enough attention. He didn't want to leave so soon and stayed for weeks, taking off with a girlfriend to one of the islands, playing tennis with Elizabeth, sitting alone in his room, sipping Chivas and watching the sun blaze out over Manila Bay one last time.

But Elizabeth was just beginning her tour, and did not take a break. She filed stories every day, sometimes fading out, falling asleep while we talked on the phone on my mornings, her nights. She was up at six and out the door by seven, dashing back to her room, her skin smudged from street fumes and grime, to write and file a piece and run out again, living twelve hours ahead of us on the East Coast. She drank mango juice and played her cassette tapes and had chunks of papaya for breakfast, margaritas at dusk. The hotel staff knew her by now, and her margaritas came perfectly timed, straight up, with a twist, salt on the rim.

Perched at the desk in her hotel room, hands flapping in time to the music, she could forget everything, doing the two things she loved most, writing and drinking.

Just around this time, her husband was planning to fly to Manila, and she had been warding off the day. We had talked about it and argued about it. I was impatient, but she wanted to be sure and worried about her parents' reaction and overturning her life, all of it. But she could not hold out any hope of reconciliation. She was struggling, she said, to break it off with dignity and grace. Elizabeth always wanted smooth endings, muted tones, and polite goodbyes.

His arrival in Manila took away her sense of having a place that was her own, as if his presence in her room violated her, she told me. She was angry that he persisted, refusing to call it off. When the moment came over dinner, it was swift. She took off her wedding band and, without saying a word, left the table. The next day he flew home. She cried on the phone, telling me about it. The plans she had meticulously plotted out—work, marriage, maybe children—were now over. Everything in her life was changing so rapidly. There was nothing easy about this, having to tell her parents and facing the truth about us, about herself, something that defied definition.

I was restless, distracted from friends and work. Gone were my fourteen-hour days, the late-night TV news from Manila, the excitement, and although the Philippines had stayed on the front pages, my involvement with the story was running its course. Tim was coming back, and he would have gladly kept me around his house, but I had to finish the things I had left undone: I had

to sell my house in the suburbs and move a truckload of furniture, rugs, books, lamps, the things one accumulates over years. I
rented a restored third-floor walkup in a riverside neighborhood
of narrow cobblestone streets and historic brick buildings. I had
a fireplace and windows overlooking a parking lot, warehouses,
and tar roofs. I moved the furniture from my house in the suburbs, where the grass had grown for months and the For Sale sign
had fallen. I had the yard mowed and the house cleaned inside
out and the For Sale sign put back up. I fixed up my city apartment, arranged my books, put up the pictures, and had a friend
set up the stereo. After work, I stopped at the frou-frou takeout
shop around the corner to pick up a fat slice of lasagna, a con-
tainer of pasta primavera, a bottle of Soave white. Occasionally
I spent an evening out with friends, in Chinatown or in Italian
restaurants or at riverside bars. Friends coddled me, kept track.

Tim had gone on another short-term assignment, and with
him gone, his pal Andy took me under his wing. He fixed great
margaritas — this much José Cuervo and triple sec in a shaker, a
cold glass, salt on the rim, twist of lime. He was fastidious about
these things. We drank outdoors in the chill of evening in his
tiny backyard, or we would go out and splurge on good wine.
Andy was a rakish figure at the newspaper, lean and handsome,
with spiky black hair, a thatch of premature gray dropping over
his forehead. He wore skinny leather ties, carried a hiker's back-
pack, and had the strong, silent manner of much older men. He
was a loner, flying off to Haiti or Salvador or Nicaragua on a moment's notice. His passport, his oversize duffel, and his "Trash
80," the Tandy TRS-80 miniature computer the paper loaned
to foreign correspondents, were always packed and ready to go.

I met him, like so many others, through Tim, when we were bowling one night across the river, over in a crass honkytonk. His posture struck me, a flat six feet, dangling arms, barbered hair shaved too high up his neck. He was broken up over a girl, living alone with his cat and the worms he grew in the basement of the place he rented on a dead-end block of ten-foot-wide tenement apartments occupied by aging hippies, freelancers, and tweedy university professors.

Andy was one of the hotshots, the sort you kept your eye on, going places. He had been assigned to cover the revolt in Haiti and had been there for weeks, but when the large moment came, the fall of Jean Claude "Baby Doc" Duvalier, the ruinous son of the longtime dictator François "Papa Doc" Duvalier, Andy missed it because the Foreign Desk had grown impatient and ordered him to fly back. Andy was holed up at a Miami airport hotel the night Baby Doc and his people fled on an airplane for France. In a fury, Andy called me to rant. He had missed the big story! Within hours he found a flight back to Port-au-Prince and arrived just in time for the riots, the fires on the streets, the mobs in the slum of Cité Soleil. When he came home weeks later, he was deeply tanned and gaunt, wearing a Liberté T-shirt. He brought me a bottle of Rhum Barbancourt, Haiti's finest. We drank it slowly, molten gold burning our throats.

You're letting your hair grow, he noticed one day over dinner. That happens after a tragedy, he said, wise man of twenty-seven, his eyes crinkling. He was talking about my long-gone relationship, the lover I had left months earlier, but I didn't tell him the truth, that no, it wasn't that — it was Elizabeth.

But he was right about one thing. I had lost direction.

I didn't go to work early. I didn't scan the news wires. I walked down the familiar hallways to the cafeteria and noticed no one. Nothing penetrated. But I still edited Elizabeth's pieces. She was finding her ground, talking out the stories with me. When she was tired after days with little sleep, I would nudge her, trying to fish out of her a curious detail, maybe a strong quote, or a sharp observation to tie up loose ends. Doing this over time, I couldn't tell where her style, the distinctive way in which she usually phrased things, left off and mine began.

The mail pouch to the Philippines went out once a week, crammed with messages, clippings, books, notepads, batteries, and when no one was paying attention I would hand our clerk a letter for Elizabeth, the envelope sealed, glued, and taped. The letters would get to Manila faster by DHL pouch than by ordinary mail. The clerk never asked questions, her eyes discreetly turned away when she took the letter and stuffed it in the bag. She watched out for messages that Elizabeth would send directly to my computer and alerted me before anyone else could notice.

But I thought everyone knew, and I didn't care.

Now it was March, and her letters came to my new apartment. I would run up the stairs, grab a beer or open a bottle of wine, dump my things on the coffee table, and rip open her mail, reading her letters in order, like chapters in a novel. She sent me a new tape, Manila Blues volume 2 — Diana Ross, Chrissie Hynde, Stevie Nicks. A large brown envelope came another day with a package of postcards — poolside at the Manila Hotel, the tennis courts, the tower wing, on which she drew arrows pointing to her room. She included election souvenirs, Marcos banners, a Cory doll, and a grainy picture of her taken in an instant-photo booth on a Manila street. I imagined her voice and imagined her in bare feet, twisting her half-smoked cigarette in the ashtray, the butt mashed on the rim, cassette tapes thrown around her on the floor, and the music coming off her boom box so loud, you could hear it down the hotel corridor.

Some nights I would go alone to a restaurant down the street where people went for tacos and music. I drank margaritas and wrote on napkins, notes I would sometimes mail her. I would leave late, ambling along those dank city streets and falling asleep on the sofa.

All that time I had been making up stories, pages I mailed to her that she would return marked up in brown ink, checkmarks along the passages she particularly liked.

She once asked me, Why do you hate it, why do you hate the place you come from? These pages were stories about the towns of my childhood in Puerto Rico, with garish cinderblock build-ings, the turquoise buildings you see all over Latin America, and the noise that fills the spaces in all those towns, the noise of people who explain their lives on the street, in bar corners, at the drugstore, the noise of infinite poverty, an impolite noise, a noise I wanted to forget.

I wrote about my father's house in a small town on the island, a large thirty- or forty-year-old house where we lived while my father had a private practice and ran the town's only hospital. Those were the years before I went away to boarding school in Pennsylvania, before my mother left him, taking all five children with her on the day she discovered he had another woman. It was a house of many rooms. The town people called it the doctor's house, imposing, rising over the town plaza. It had tile floors and a sloping corrugated tin roof and five terraces. I wrote about the maids who cooked our meals and cleaned the house, and my mother in her heels and her perfume, a lawyer from the big city, San Juan, waiting all night for my father to come home, her eyes black stones.

I went away the year I was fourteen, my trunk packed with sweaters and woolen skirts, my name on labels stitched in each. I was flying off to a place I could scarcely imagine, a private school in the Philadelphia countryside, set among groves of trees, horse stables, and hockey fields. Something happened to me there. At first I was intimidated and shy living among girls older and taller and worldlier than I, the only Latin American, two thousand miles from home and family. I longed for my mother's voice, for my sisters and my aunt and my grandmother, everything and everyone I had grown up with. Every morning I awoke nauseated, with an ache, a hole in me. But with time I fell in love with the school and wrote poems and began to dream, think, and write home in English. When I returned to Puerto Rico for the summer holidays — having seen snow, pristine green farmlands, and big houses with great lawns and people who didn't raise their voices — I was uncomfortable. Returning to my mother's house, a home she rented in San Juan after she left my father, I lay in bed, hearing her sobs from down the hallway, hating my father and longing for the tranquility of my days in boarding school, when the real world hardly ever penetrated. But I was in Puerto Rico, dressing up in lace and silk, in crinolines, to please

my mother. I was a debutante dancing the nights away with tux-
edoed boys who smelled of cologne and brought me gardenias.

When I was nineteen, out of college, I lived in a walkup in
Brooklyn, telling myself this was the place where I would write
my books. I worked as a proofreader in Greenwich Village,
making a show of reading Camus on the job and sitting on a
bench alone in Washington Square Park in the winter sun. I had
to cross Fourteenth Street to get the subway home. I used to hate
that walk from the office on Fifth Avenue to Fourteenth Street.
I cringed at the sight of tacky stores stacked up with cheap merchandise, fleshy girls in tight skirts and spike heels, smacking
gum, and loud men with skinny mustaches and greasy hair.
Boom boxes played mambos and merengues at full volume and
people greeted each other, screaming, on the sidewalks. *"¡Ay,
muchacha, cómo te va?"* Embarrassed at this coarse display, I
would pretend I didn't understand Spanish, that I was not from
Puerto Rico, but every now and then I stopped at the alcapurria
stand and got a couple of rolls, a taste I remembered so well, and
ate them on the way home.

Elizabeth thought I was stronger for this, what she called my
circumstances. Hers were quite different. Everything in her life,
she said, had been either "a straight shot to glory"—a phrase
she used often, mostly in mockery—with the right schooling,
polished manners, and a sense of entitlement, or "a straight road
to hell," which included passion, books, writing, bourbon in the
night. For a long time, she had tried to live an agnostic, neutral
life, exquisitely modulated, cocktails precisely at seven, Spode
china on the dining table, a perfect dog, a perfect house, a perfect

marriage. Her fear of letting herself go, of loving anyone she wanted, was deep in her, deeper than I knew.

That's why you may not want to come to Manila, she warned me. It's up to you, she said, but this isn't friendship. "It's something dreadful and brilliant."

3

I ARRIVED IN MANILA in late March, after a thirty-hour flight spent squeezed in a window seat in economy. On the way from the East Coast to Los Angeles, I read a book, smoked, drank wine, and paced up and down the aisles. For years I wouldn't fly anywhere, and there I was flying halfway around the world. We had a five-hour layover in Los Angeles in the middle of the night, and, relieved that at least one leg of the trip was over, I had a beer in the terminal, wandered around the airport shops, and with nothing else to do, tried to get some sleep, bundling myself on a bench, but it was impossible.

Filipinos swarmed around the check-in counters, a mass of people with bulging suitcases and overflowing shopping bags and large cardboard boxes strung with rope. It seemed a whole country was moving. I had seen this before, at the Miami airport, at the gates for Caribbean and Central American flights. It reminded me of flights from San Juan on Pan American clippers flying to Miami and New York with laborers and farmhands crowded in the back of the plane, women holding on to their babies, men in straw peasant hats holding on to shopping bags of beans, plantains, and mangoes.

The Philippine Airlines flight was packed, an airborne migrant bus. For the thousands of Filipinos making a living in California, it was the cheapest way home. Once all were aboard the Boeing 747, the PAL flight turned into a fiesta. We got as much San Miguel beer as we could drink, had meals every other hour, and could smoke anywhere. There were loud gatherings in the aisles, in the galleys, by the exit doors. In that setting there was no room for solitude or reflection. I had five hours before the stopover in Honolulu and another ten or twelve, depending on the headwinds, before landing in Manila. The movies flickered silently on the screen, people wrapped in smelly blankets snored, and the cabin was freezing, while the attendants, young Filipinas with fluttering eyelashes and whispery voices, giggled in the curtained-off kitchen galleys.

I couldn't sleep and pretended I was already living in Manila time. I tried to picture Elizabeth's day. Was she watching the clock, counting the hours until my arrival? Forty-five thousand feet above the Pacific, in the predawn dark, a vast blackness out there, I couldn't see her face anymore, couldn't hear her voice. She had become evanescent, a hallucination, a blur of reddish gold, ivory, and cream, the shades of her.

It was early morning in Honolulu when we landed for refueling. Strange all of a sudden to see daylight and palm trees, and to have flown back in time. Hawaii seemed a mirage suspended between yesterday and tomorrow, a few thousand miles east of the International Date Line, dead time, when in a second, you lose a whole day of your life.

The last leg of the trip was the longest, twelve sleepless hours.

I was jammed against a couple of seatmates, a disheveled girl in a frayed frock who was playing nurse to the obese fellow she was traveling with, feeding him his meals, tucking him into the blanket, taking him to the bathroom. He had hired her in San Francisco to keep him company on his bride-hunting trip to the Philippines. He had documents, pictures, and letters from a girl there, he said, and I thought of that poor Filipina, dreaming of a handsome Americano and a house in the California suburbs.

The smell of stale food, waste, and sweat filled the cabin, and my legs ached, but I was distracted, listening to the Filipina attendants talk up the wonders of their country, the volcanoes, the mountain ranges, the beaches of Boracay. Finally we descended through miles of rain clouds and then broke through. I looked down on a gray sea and the dirt-sand coastline of Manila, narrow-tailed boats, fishing nets strung from black poles, wobbly shacks partly immersed in water, and everywhere, from one end to the other, palm trees. Just as I had imagined. I felt a sudden quickening in my chest and jumped to grab my bags, first in line.

After all that distance and time, it now seemed there had been no distance at all between the East Coast, thirteen time zones away, and this haunting country.

The Manila airport sat in a bayside field surrounded by shacks. In 1981, when it was completed, it had a sleek, modern look, a sweep of steel and concrete and sheaths of glass. But in 1986, just five years later, the exterior looked weather-beaten, and the cream-colored linoleum corridors were scuffed, smelling of industrial cleaner and cigarette smoke. I moved down the terminal in a fog from jet lag and the shock of arrival, my duffels banging against my legs. As we came to Immigration, a row of cubicles with uniformed clerks eating their lunch of garlic rice and longanisa, the smell of pork sausages drifting to the passenger queue, a mariachi band appeared, plucking away at string guitars. Dazed, I smiled at everyone. *Mabuhay!*

I looked for Elizabeth but knew she would not be there. She would think it too ordinary to come greet me at the airport. Or perhaps she was frightened of some public display—that I would run to her and grab her in my arms. But for hundreds of others these arrivals were a celebration, and they crowded against waist-high barricades, shouting and shoving to embrace friends and relatives.

Elizabeth had sent a driver to pick me up, and there he was, holding up a cardboard sign with my name carefully printed on it. He had a rubbery face and eyes puffy from heavy drinking. Outside, on the ramp for arrivals, the multitudes multiplied and the temperature seemed twenty degrees hotter. The sunlight made red motes in my eyes, my skin felt grainy, dozens of minuscule bumps rose on my neck. The muscles in my arms twitched, blood rushed to my face. I put on my sunglasses, hoping the circles under my eyes would not show, and ran my hands through my hair, which was curling in the heat. Buzzing around us were hordes of vendors, cabdrivers, guards blowing whistles, flower peddlers. There was no room to move. The taxis were battered, the fenders dented if they had fenders at all. The seats were covered in torn clear plastic or in heavy corduroy. Flowers wrapped in cellophane were thrust at my face from every side, and sampanguita garlands were flung around my neck. "Mum,

mum, you want?" vendors whined, holding out palms with filthy fingernails. "Only one peso, please, mum."

Rolly, my driver, shooed them away and went to get his car. Shoved by the crowd, I waited for him to come around, wilting in the humidity and the stink. Out beyond the airport, they were burning rubber tires, garbage, and sewage, a nauseating smell I would come to always identify with the country. The heat had a meanness to it. Like a swamp. No sweet breezes off the bay, no swaying palm trees, no bright tropical flowers. Only this suffocating damp heat and the bitter smell of too many bodies packed too tightly in airless space.

The road that ran from the airport to downtown Manila followed the contours of the bay. It was lined with dying palm trees, squatter camps, unfinished condos, discos, fleabag motels, cocktail lounges, fish markets, churches, massage parlors, and food stands. A long time ago the road was the boulevard of the rich, with their mansions facing the harbor and the iridescent sunsets of the South China Sea. Roxas Boulevard was hardly grand now, but there was still a touch of lost beauty in the sweep of the road, the panorama of the bay, and even in the frayed royal palm trees along the way.

As we lurched from light to light, bumping over potholes in insane traffic, Rolly pointed out the sights. The Baclaran Cathedral, the Manila Yacht Club, the Metropolitan Museum of the Philippines. The sky was a primal blue, cloudless, and the sun was bristling on that twenty-second of March, at the peak of the dry season. I rolled down the car window to smell the city, inhaling the fumes from the jeepneys that crisscrossed lanes, blasting their horns. The jeepneys, jitney buses converted from discarded wartime jeeps, were the main public transport on the Philippine islands, tailor-made to suit the owner and christened with names like Sagittarius, Sweetheart, Virgin Mary, and dolled up with gaudy lights, heart-shaped decals, ribbons, and Child Christ figurines dangling off the rearview mirror.

At an intersection on the bayside, on a landfill jutting into the harbor, a cluster of boxy mausoleum-like buildings were laid out on watered lawns between tree-lined boulevards, slums and sari-sari stores, roadside stands selling cigarettes and beer. The buildings had the impersonal presence of American convention halls. These constituted Imelda's monument to herself, the campus of the Cultural Center of the Philippines. Rolly beamed at the sight. To him it looked American, like pictures he had seen of Los Angeles. Imelda had it built in the 1960s to lure international conferences and jet-set glitter to these bedraggled shores. In the 1970s celebrities the world over did come to the brocade ballrooms to be wined and dined under vaulted ceilings and chandeliers. Ronald and Nancy Reagan flew in for a visit, as did the fringe Hollywood stars, the George Hamiltons and Liberaces, and the heiresses and divorcées, the Doris Dukes and Christina Fords. Now the Cultural Center was drawing only the has-beens of the concert circuit, itinerant evangelists, and third-rate conventions.

Rolly tried to be the perfect guide, and I was absorbed, already defining the place, and watching for the Manila Hotel. First I saw the tower wing, a vertical white concrete rectangle with a slanting bluish-green roof. As we got closer, driving past the iron gates of the whitewashed American embassy, where dozens of Filipinos shoved and slept in line to apply for visas, I saw the hotel of Elizabeth's postcards. And I felt the blood pounding in my head, knowing that she was waiting.

The hotel was elegant, vintage 1912 California missionary style, set back from the street with a sweeping driveway and a porte-cochère edged with royal palm trees. It was painted a colonial white, and it had turrets and balconies and floor-to-ceiling casement windows. General MacArthur had lived there for years; Hemingway had visited. In 1986 the hotel was the province of the foreign press. U.S. networks and newspapers all had offices there. Diplomats and congressmen, human rights activists, freelancers, and photographers roamed the halls. Informants, treasure hunters, and Vietnam War veterans lazed around in the hotel bars, drinking Johnnie Walker in mahogany-paneled rooms fragrant with fresh orchids.

I didn't want to hurry as I stepped up through the brass-framed portal, walking under the high swooping arches past bellboys in white uniforms, gliding on marble floors that glistened from decades of polish. I was trembling, seized by a sickening sensation of terror and excitement, but tried to appear casual, like a jaded tourist landing at yet another port. The lobby was enormous, with clusters of dark burgundy sofas and armchairs laid out under a carved wooden ceiling and cascading Capiz chandeliers.

It was a hotel for grand entrances and passionate intrigues, drunken reveries and moonlight dinners by the water. I could see myself growing old in those rooms, having coffee by the pool every morning. I would become an eccentric character in a straw hat and sunglasses, wandering absent-mindedly through the garden. "She comes here every Christmas," the regulars would whisper. "She has her Bombay at that table at six o'clock every day. They say she writes books."

Rolly took my bags to the shiny marble-gray reception desk, where the carefully groomed clerks chirped and laughed, greeting me effusively by name. They had everything ready, the registration form, the bay-view room, a formal letter of welcome. A manager took me up to my room, and I knew Elizabeth was near, not there in my room on the eleventh floor, but in room 817, where she had been living for two months, where she worked and played music, the room I had tried to picture so often.

Taking his time, the manager offered me chilled fresh kalamansi juice, a bowl of tropical fruit—mangoes, papaya, bananas—and a bouquet of flowers plucked from the hotel's garden. He threw open the dark wooden trellis that had been placed in front of the sliding glass doors to keep the sunlight from bleaching the upholstery. Through the glass doors to a small balcony, I looked out on the harbor and the pool and garden below. I stood there for a minute, squinting at the sun, forgetting the manager was still in the room.

On the bed was a plain paper bag with my name on it, in Elizabeth's handwriting. After the manager left, I tore it open. I pulled out a T-shirt with an Asian woman's face printed on its front, a small bag of salty plantain chips—the kind I loved as a child—a Philippines flag decal, and a hardcover notebook with

a scrawled note on the opening page, *Mabuhay Ang Filipinas!*
Figured you'd find something to fill this up—Elizabeth. I sat on
the bed, tried on the T-shirt. I took the adhesive paper off the
decal and pasted it on the notebook's red cardboard front cover.
I opened the bag of plantains and took a mouthful. I sipped kalamansi juice: tart, like lime, but with a sweet edge. I took a quick
shower, rinsing the plane off me, and put on jeans and a shirt. I
looked in the mirror. My face had no color; my hands shook.

Finally I walked down the hallway, past the guard, to the elevator and punched 8, and walked very, very slowly to her door.
I knocked and she opened immediately, the sudden click star-
tling me. I stood there, frozen. The sun beamed in on the room,
streaking her hair. Her face was fuller and her skin was shades
darker, deeply tanned, and she was smiling, gleaming in a way
I had not seen her before. Everything I had thought about, the
words I would say, the way I had scripted this moment, all of it
left me. I stared at her, whispering something. I don't know what
we said but we didn't touch.

Walking in, I flopped down in a rattan armchair and she took
the sofa. She inspected me closely, getting used to my being
there, stretching her legs the length of the sofa. "Your hair's
long." She smiled, her eyes running over me. "But you look
great." I could feel every pore on my skin, every line on my
face. I looked around the room. Brown furniture, rust colors,
vanilla walls. She had a Philippines flag on a wall—dark blue,
white, and red with a sunburst of yellow—a Cory doll, bumper
stickers and banners from the campaign. Messages, notes, and
postcards were stuck with pushpins on a board above her desk.

She had her Walkman wired to hand-size speakers on top of a TV set, her Tandy computer on the desk next to her old Royal typewriter. There were clothes draped on a chair. The sliding door to the balcony, which the housekeepers liked to keep locked against flies and mosquitoes, was wide open.

She brought me a drink and took one of my cigarettes. I couldn't look straight at her, and the tension didn't ease as we talked and drank wine. Neither of us moved. At last she rose to refill her glass and walked behind me. I could feel her standing very close behind me, her hand on my shoulder, and I touched it, keeping my hand on hers for a very long time.

That evening we went to a café in the Ermita-Mabini neighborhood they called "the tourist district." We took a sidewalk table under a Cinzano umbrella and drank wine and picked at gambas al ajillo. Children were playing hopscotch and jumping rope across the street on Remedios Circle, and vendors strolled by with bunches of red roses and carnations. Table candles flickered in the breeze, and the night was bright with the headlights of passing taxis and the neon signs of restaurants and nightclubs and cocktail lounges. Café Adriatico was packed and noisy, and the bells of the four-hundred-year-old Malate Church tolled nearby.

"*Es un gran festival,*" Elizabeth said, radiant. There was something startlingly different about her. She didn't sit with her arms crossed tightly around her chest. She didn't stiffen her jaw. She seemed younger, talking freely, laughing loudly, her dimples rippling around her mouth. We talked about everything: early years, moments, Manila, her work, my work, and writing. Interrupting me, she would speak in Spanish, as if the language itself were ours only.

I had gotten no sleep in more than forty-eight hours, had lost a day in transit, but the soreness from the flight, and the weariness, were gone, as if I had crossed no distance at all and the passage of time itself, the two long months we had been apart, were abruptly reduced to a day or two. But at the same time everything was different.

For once I didn't feel foreign, an outsider consciously reshaping myself to fit in. Foreign places, especially untamed tropical islands, can give you that fleeting sensation of total freedom. It is their ultimate appeal, the illusion that one can be entirely oneself, without bounds and conventions, a pilgrim soul stopping by on the way to nowhere.

That evening, with the vendors bringing us roses and the air filled with chattering voices, I thought I had found a home. Elizabeth was leaning back on the rickety metal chair one moment and lurching forward the next, her lips red from the wine, her eyes fixated on me. She was an apparition, an invention of mine, perhaps.

We let the evening stretch, in no hurry to leave our spot under the umbrella, letting the spicy chicken get cold and ordering more wine, her foot touching mine, her fingers darting over my hand. In time we climbed into a taxi back to the hotel, rolling down the windows, her hair blowing into her eyes as the taxi sped down Roxas Boulevard and the city and the bay around us flashed by, all lights.

We stayed up a long time in her room, watching the red lights

of the freighters in the bay and the torches sputtering in the garden below, her tape deck running for hours in the dark, Bach's
Air, Pachelbel's Canon, Albinoni's Adagio, the same tape playing over and over.

When I awoke the next morning she was gone. I had coffee,
read the papers, showered. I thought I had all the time in the
world. An hour passed before she appeared. She was sweating
and flushed, her ponytail curling, drenched, her shorts and T-
shirt soaked. She had jogged around Rizal Park near the hotel
and up to the Cultural Center and looked wrung out. But there
was something else in her face, a troubled look.

What's wrong, I asked, getting up from the sofa and going to
her. She looked away. Gently turning her face back to me, I saw
she was crying, her mouth twisted, choking back sobs. I tried to
hold her but she pushed me away. She couldn't do this, she said
quietly. She had to go back to her husband, do the right thing
and live the kind of life she had planned.

I couldn't believe it. All of it struck me at once. I could hardly
speak. My head was pounding, and I wanted to scream. I felt as if
I were in a play, something unreal, that the moment would soon
pass. How could so much change in a few hours, from night to
day? Was this what she had tried to warn me against—herself?

She crumpled on the sofa, her body in a small bundle on a
corner, heaving with wrenching sobs. Seeing her like that, her
words echoing in my head, I was suddenly in a rage that began
small and deep and then exploded. I had been given four weeks
of vacation, only four weeks, not much time, all of it now crashing around me.

Give me four weeks, I pleaded. Give me four weeks.

I turned my back on her and stepped on the balcony and stood looking down, wanting to scream, my eyes blurring. I was gripping the balcony rail, looking down and away to the bay. I was desperate. I knew what she was up against. I remembered my anguish and fear, a gnashing depression and shame during those awful college years when I feared that fingers were pointed at me, when taboo words were whispered and a stigma attached to girls with buzzcuts, muscled arms and legs, and athletic swaggers. I was not like them. I wore skirts and lipstick and didn't have an athletic bone in my body. I lied for years to my mother, my family, my friends and classmates and the wet-mouthed boys and men I dated into my late twenties. These weren't outright lies. These were omissions, half-truths, avoidance. I tried to live two lives and fooled only a few. But I didn't get married like my mother had hoped. I did not live the life I was bred to live. Elizabeth was boxed in, trapped in a marriage she no longer could fulfill. I don't know how long I clung to the rail there, wanting to disappear, until she came behind me, quietly wrapping her arms around me, saying nothing.

We stayed in the room that day, sorting out our lives. There was little about us that had been preordained, little that would have signaled our attraction. On the face of it, ours was less a melding of like-minded spirits than a collision of immutable forces: her steely reserve and rigorous emotional discipline and my obsessive passion and combustible temperament. But there we were, unable to let go of each other. I can't remember if it was that day or some other time when she asked about my love affairs. She forced a laugh here and there, calling me Lothario, counting with the fingers of one hand the number of affairs I had left in shambles behind me. Hers was a lean life. She had her boyfriend, met him in college, lived with him a few years, got engaged and married, and was now leaving him. She hadn't counted on me showing up in her life.

We watched the sun bleach the sky at midday and watched it grow into a giant orange ball as it sank into the bay at dusk. After the hours alone, talking, crying, I began to know the fear she lived with. It was the fear of us together.

Mornings by the pool, lounging alone, getting darker and younger, sipping green mango juice and reading, lying under the yellowing leaves of the banyan trees, making up stories in my head, scribbling in my red notebook, filling the pages. That winter in Tim's house, those days when I awoke startled and gagged in the bathroom, the empty house in the suburbs, the old miscast relationship—all of it faded away in Manila. Those mornings by the pool with my books, and the late afternoons in my hotel room on the eleventh floor, writing on a clunky, battered pink-lacquered typewriter I bought in a pawnshop in Manila, were the first moments of peace I had known in a long time.

We were up soon after dawn every morning, Elizabeth charging around, gathering pens, highlighters, notepads, tape recorder, and camera, and bolting out the door, late for an appointment. I had the day ahead of me. I was on vacation. I had nothing scheduled. In my first few days I had Rolly drive me around, shopping trips for cheap Reeboks and discount Ralph Lauren shirts. We drove around the gated, walled-off residential areas, peering up to mansions not unlike in size and opulence to those in Beverly Hills, and we stepped into the sewer-filthy alleys in the garbage slum of Tondo. All through town kids crowded around the car when we stopped at red lights and crossed intersections, knocking on my window, their faces against the glass, their mouths opened with the pitiful cry, "Mum, mum, I'm hungry, one peso, mum." Those first few days I gave them money, and Rolly would look at me and shake his head. "They are gangs. Don't give them money," he said every time. He kept his window rolled up and his door locked. After a while I forced myself to turn away from the begging kids, locking my car door and rolling up my window when we stopped at an intersection.

I had Rolly take me to Camp Aguinaldo, the military headquarters where the revolution had started, where the nuns had stopped Marcos's tanks. The entrance gate hung off its hinges and the thick stone and cinderblock walls were pockmarked with mortar shells and bullets. We drove by Malacañang Palace, the presidential palace that was once the residence of the American governor in the period from 1898 to 1946 when the United States governed the Philippines, but these days the palace was overrun with street vendors, beggars, and tourists.

Manila was euphoric that spring. A month after the revolution, everyone was still partying. There were street fiestas, Catholic masses, and lavish dinners in the mansions of Cory's wealthy supporters. Everywhere they played the sad melody

"Bayan Ko," a national ballad that had been Cory's campaign anthem.

> *Philippines! My heart's sole burning fire,*
> *Cradle of my tears . . .*

The woman at the beauty salon in the Manila Hotel, who cut my hair the first Sunday I was in town, kept asking me, as did everyone else: "Do you like our country? Did you see it on TV?" For once, Filipinos were no longer seen worldwide as the maids, menial laborers, and whores of Asia. After so many demeaning years, they became television stars, protagonists in the People Power Revolution.

Cory Aquino had not moved into Malacañang Palace. It was too full of ghosts: those dim and musty halls, the baroque furniture, the remnants of Ferdinand and Imelda Marcos. As soon as the Marcos cohort was forced to leave, the palace was swamped with vendors and vagrants. At one point, Cory spoke seriously of turning it into a love motel for honeymooners. Poor families set up huts inside the palace's gates, cooking while tourists strolled around. Youngsters sold revolution trinkets and merchants set up stalls around the palace with mementos, keys, visors, straw hats, and T-shirts ("People Power Is God Power" was popular). Tourists queued up for hours in the heat to tour Malacañang—the dark rooms, the basement disco, the secret clinic with Marcos's oxygen tank, and, of course, the closets of Imelda's shoes, her bottles of French perfume and shelves of Hermès and Vuitton bags and silky lingerie.

The city was a bazaar, mayhem, with slums everywhere,

even around Malacañang. I had expected the poverty, but not the veneer of prosperity, the ersatz Americanization. Rows of pricey Miami-type condominiums lined the avenues of Makati, a wealthy district where the capital's stock market and top corporations had their headquarters. There were fancy residential enclaves where the only people on the streets I saw were maids in uniforms and gardeners clipping the grassy strips on the sidewalks. Villas with tennis courts and swimming pools were kept safe from the rabble by surly uniformed guards armed with M16s and by twelve-foot-high concrete walls topped with razor wire. Inside the gates of the mansions, Mercedes Benzes and MGs, Porsches and Ford SUVs, lined the driveways, and there were household staffs large enough to run small hotels. But the slums were beginning to encroach on Makati and the homes of the rich, and the paint was peeling off some of the old mansions; people were afraid to go out at night.

By my second week at the hotel, guests had come and gone. A few stayed longer and became fixtures in the scenery. There was the woman in the red spandex swimsuit, with the tended body, the sort of woman who travels to a remote spa in the Alps to have her skin stretched out just so. Easy to see her in thick gold bangles and Oscar de la Renta gowns, her hair bleached and stiff like a wig, swept up in a French twist. She held her body tight, and her face had the shrunken look of years of dieting. She stretched out her leathery legs, rubbing them against each other, while her back reclined on the chaise longue directly under the sun. She wore lavender-frame sunglasses and held up one hand at her forehead like a visor while the other held up one of those summer bestsellers. A flabby middle-aged guest, thin-haired and pear-shaped, turned to me one day and said, aghast, "Do you know, she's sixty!"

Most weekdays the hotel was empty. Tourism was down, and the press was out working. The waiters lolled under the shade; a few children splashed in the pool. The tennis pro, old Leo, with his oiled black hair and rolling paunch, waddled aimlessly around the clubhouse, recalling old times, checking up on new arrivals, and roughhousing with his boys, young guys who had the arms and legs to take on the toughest players. Early in the morning, right around the time the sun started glinting silver on the bay, the clubhouse crew would line up the blue and white striped loungers along the edges of the pool. They swept the grounds and skimmed fallen leaves off the water, and stacked up the tangerine towels, but aside from a few of us, no one was around.

Every now and then, Elizabeth dropped by the pool between press conferences and interviews, and lay under the prickling sun on the chair beside me, her shirtsleeves rolled up, a bandanna in her back pocket, sweat making her shirt stick to her back. She was there just a few minutes until she had to run out again, always harried. She had a long stride, her head bobbing as she trotted in a rush to get somewhere.

She didn't run with the press pack. She didn't share notes, she didn't cuddle up with them, she didn't party much, and she didn't show up when they showed up.

But she went with Nick to Cagayan province. Nick, New

Delhi Nick, whom I adored and indulged those first years on the
Foreign Desk when he was reporting from India and Thailand,
from Bhopal and Srinagar and Bangkok. Now he was in Manila,
reigning over the press corps from his office on the second floor
of the Manila Hotel, handing out chilled beer bottles from his
minibar, along with free tips on life in Manila and recycled war
stories. He had left me messages as soon as he heard I was in
Manila and now was taking me out to dinner at La Taverna, a
favorite hangout of the *farang*, the expats, a grungy place with
dusty Chianti bottles lined up on wooden beams around the dining area. Italian flags and posters hung on streaky stucco walls.

We relived the old days and caught up on our lives (his divorce, my breakup) when midway through the antipasto he
mentioned Elizabeth—he called her Whitney. Clearing his
throat, a sure sign that unpleasantness was coming, he shifted
his body, pulling up the chair closer to me. "She's stuck up, isn't
she, a bit of a pill," he said, his mustache wet from the wine, his
eyes a little glassy, red rimmed. He was now peering closely at
me, trying to size up my reaction, and he snapped open his silver
Zippo and flicked up a flame for both of our cigarettes. "She's
like tear gas, toxic."

I felt the sting, and said something inane in return, swallow-
ing hard. He had no idea how it hurt, or why. But I knew she had
that effect on some reporters who went up against her—not all,
but enough of them to isolate her. She seemed awkward with the
gang at the hotel bar where we all put together tables and drank
for hours. It was a rite, everyone showing off for each other. But
I thought she had to strain to fit in, and it made me uncomfort-

able for her. "She's no good in groups," I admitted, but didn't agree that her aloof pose meant that she was cold and indifferent. I told Nick he should get to know her. She's not all that bad, I said, laughing. Later that evening, back in her room, I told her what he had said. Maybe I shouldn't have told her. She stood stock-still, glaring at me, but said nothing. I knew it hurt her; her silence said it all.

A few days later she went with Nick to Cagayan, a hellhole in northern Luzon where the communists had a stronghold. When she came back two days later, cranky and dirty, her clothes coated with dust, she went straight to the bathroom to wash up. I knew she was fuming. She had stepped into his old job and chafed at Nick's overbearing shadow, his swagger, his boisterous confidence, boyish ego, and rough edges. Going along with Nick was her concession to me, and a friendly gesture to him. But the trip to Cagayan had done nothing to change her mind. She didn't like working with other reporters. She didn't like having to listen to their war stories. She wanted to work alone.

We argued about this. I thought she had to try to work with others, to go out and have a beer or two, to share a few stories. I believed that once she relaxed, everyone would love her. It bothered me that they didn't, that they didn't see in her what I saw. I wanted her to stroll into the Lobby Lounge, drop her bag on the floor, snap her fingers for a gin and tonic, and tell her stories. But that was me. I would sit around the table in the Lobby Lounge, or by the pool, in a crowd of a dozen veteran reporters, and speak out blithely, as if I had been in the Philippines all my life, as if I knew anything.

She joined occasionally, pulling up a chair away from the center of the crowd and draining her drink, her eyes wandering, half listening or not listening at all, absently playing with her pen. She had just dropped into town, a novice from the suburbs, and was terrified by her ignorance, her lack of experience. At the same time she was relentless, blitzing through the city, tossing off routine news, finding stories others had overlooked. But in the end, she and the rest of the crowd were all covering the same ground.

There were weekends in the months of upheaval that followed the fall of Marcos when a riot would erupt at a rally of Marcos's *abandonados*, and the press, sunning by the hotel pool, would rise from their towels and jump into long pants to go cover it. The rallies had a pattern. Two thousand people, hard-core Marcos believers, massed every Sunday around a stage at the Luneta, the grandstand at Rizal Park, a stone's throw from the hotel. Speeches, wailing prayers, and Imelda's teary songs, taped in exile in Honolulu, began at dawn, waking the hotel guests. Looking over the hedges, we could keep track of the rally and the riot police in their helmets and Dirty Harry shades, swinging their long, wooden batons. Most days there was just posturing. But violence could break out abruptly. Sometimes people were injured, killed.

That's when the press would leap from poolside chairs, charge out of the hotel, and run across the park, Elizabeth, her notebook and pen in hand, her running shoes untied, her hair tumbling. I would stay by the pool or wander off into the park, staying on the fringes, not quite knowing what to do with my-

self, neither reporter nor tourist, feeling left out, rather useless.
Late at night she would return to the hotel, drenched in sweat
and stinking of tear gas, her bandanna twisted around her neck.

Sunday mornings were a ritual. The press was out in full force.
Early risers came in tennis whites, holding Prince rackets under their arms. Late risers came out with bloodshot eyes from
Saturday night's barhopping in Ermita, all-nighters of knocking back six-packs and sleazing around the strip. By noon the
poolside tables buzzed with chatter. Twenty people shouting,
beer bottles piling up. "Boss, boss," Nick screamed at the waiters, who moved in prissy steps and paid no attention. Beers were
easy. Piña coladas required extensive instructions. No sugar, and
just this much foam, two fingers, and the waiter invariably responded, "No problem, mum." Half an hour later the piña co-
lada arrived in a tall, warm glass, a sugary mix with five fingers
of foam topping it off. The piña coladas, sold by the dozen, were
swallowed in quick gulps, and not a drop was left in the glass,
just wisps of foam for the flies to crawl over. It was just about
this time that the hottest sun settled in a spot directly overhead
and pinned everyone down.

I am watching you—a note from Elizabeth on one of those
days when, wishing to be alone, she dragged a chair under a tree,
away from the crowd. I was propped up on my side on a lounge
chair by the pool. My hair was wet, slicked back, and my head
moved naturally back and forth while I talked to a hefty blond
fellow on the chair next to me. I ran my hand over my sweaty
thighs and legs, rubbing oil over them, and sensed that she was
watching me, could feel her eyes without looking in her direc-

tion. The fellow was turning toward me, listening. I was talking about the Philippines as usual, playing with my hair, sipping my beer. He seemed charmed, transfixed, lighting my cigarette. I inhaled slowly and let the smoke out in a long stream. I was doing this for her: I knew she was looking at me behind her sunglasses. Everything around me slowed down, the sun burned my skin, and the wind was still, the heat rising.

Some days the temperature was a perfect 85—the brochure tropics—with the wind off the South China Sea driving out the ghastly odor from the garbage in Manila Bay. The leaves of the trees became a translucent green, and the haze lifted. The sky turned a cerulean blue, just as it does in the Caribbean after midday showers.

On the day of my birthday, my second Saturday in Manila, we drove down the coast to find Matabungkay Beach. We hired a driver and rode for a couple of hours on a narrow road clogged with trucks, buses, and sputtering jeepneys. There was nothing panoramic about the drive, as people had told us there would be, no coastline to see. But we were involved with each other, barely aware of the driver and the road, until we spotted a faded billboard announcing the Matabungkay Beach Resort. We took a dirt road past shacks and beer stalls and at the end of it we found the resort, the main building a large, airy shed of concrete with a tin roof. It wasn't the enchanting pavilion, the white beaches, we had in mind, but having gone so far and having a day to ourselves, we ran up to the reception desk and signed up for a raft. Cheap, ten pesos for half a day. In the restaurant a throng of people, not the foreign tourists of the Manila Hotel but barrio

Filipinos, large, loud parties, were picnicking and drinking, the women with their heavy breasts, the men with their soft bellies.

Out in the water there were dozens of *bancas*, narrow-tailed boats, loaded with families. Vendors in cutoff shorts and rubber sandals, their skin charcoaled by the sun, their bodies fish-bony and sinewy, waded through the water, carrying boxes of food, beer, and ice cream. We hired two of them to pull our bamboo raft into the water and they anchored it about two hundred feet from the shore. A vendor took our lunch order and one hour later he was back, wading in the sea while balancing a damp box on his head with our rice, crispy fried fish, and a couple of San Miguel beers. We spread the food on a dry palm leaf and ate it with our fingers and drank the lukewarm beer.

The water was so clear, you could see the bottom. Elizabeth dived in and out, and I dangled my legs off the raft, splashing water on my face and arms to keep cool. I rarely went into the water. I only wanted to smell it, to feel it near me, to feel it like the air. I watched her body swivel, and the changing light on the waves, and the sun spots skittering under water. Around us the boats swayed, like floating huts. Kids jumped naked into the sea, teenagers danced to boom boxes, and men tossed their empty bottles over their shoulders. By midafternoon the beach became quiet, that drowsiness that comes in the tropics as the sun spreads out and mutes everything, and the boats, black silhouettes, lay still.

She stretched out on the raft to dry in the sun, her hand shading her eyes while she looked at me. We were alone in the world, it seemed, hardly stirring, swaying softly with the waves. From somewhere I thought I could hear Vivaldi's *Four Seasons*, and in the distance, looking inland beyond the shore, white wisps of smoke swirled from hillside huts and the scent of burning wood drifted back to the sea, even from that far.

I knew at that instant, with her face beside me and the wisps of smoke in the hills beyond, that I had found myself a place; nothing I had known before had captured me in quite this way, with such sudden passion. We let the last hours of the sun pass, and that evening, back in Manila, we sat under windblown torches, listening to the strolling violins in the hanging gardens by the bay.

Weeks later, when my holiday ended and I had to leave Manila, I gave Elizabeth a gold ring with a sliver of coral set in it. She wore it for a long time on her left hand.

4

I LEFT THE PHILIPPINES in early May, after the spring and the sea and the gold ring, the weeks that were her gift to me. Tearing myself away, delaying my scheduled departure once, twice, one day, then another, I finally returned to the United States, but not to stay. I was going back to end that life, to break away from the things that had once mattered: a long career, ambitions and promotions, a climb that had been steady and single-minded, but leaving me restless.

On the interminable flight from Manila, I practiced the words I would use, arranged my reasoning for public consumption, wanting to explain my decision to resign in a sensible, dispassionate manner. I tried to mimic Elizabeth's even-tempered voice in imaginary conversations in which I convinced myself that the course I was about to take was absolutely right, inevitable, handed to me that afternoon on the bamboo raft at the Matabungkay resort. I had a plan: I would quit the newspaper and return to the Philippines to write, to cover the revolution, to be with her.

It seemed simple the day I told Elizabeth. We were having drinks in the Lobby Lounge and I dropped the idea abruptly, my mind already made up. I had wanted her to back me, to take me by the hand and call for wine to celebrate. But the soft look on her face hardened. She shifted her glance away from me and her hand moved automatically to her mouth, fingers on her lips, the pose she adopted to give herself a moment to recover. She wanted to believe I was only dreaming, that this was one of those romantic creations of mine that often amused her but more often scared her. She thought this would pass, that I was carried away on palm trees and margaritas.

"You can't give up your career just like that," she said. "What if this doesn't work out, what then?" She was afraid of the burden, that the time would come when I would end up blaming her for ruining my life and that a sense of obligation would shift to her. I had answers ready, trying to reassure her, and brushed aside her arguments in a torrent of words.

On the morning I left her in her room, knowing that nothing would keep me from going back, she took me in her arms, her hands cold, as they always were when she was afraid or anxious, and clasped me to her. She seemed suddenly smaller and very alone. I had to go, and loosened her arms. She fixed her eyes somewhere in the distance, looking toward the bay. I closed the door behind me, the breath taken out of me.

Flying east to America, strapped to my seat, I played back the days and nights in Manila, the torchlights and the ships, the trenchant music, dreading going back to reality. I flew dazed and disconnected from Honolulu International to LAX. I called her from a pay phone at LAX but could hear only broken phrases. Passengers, couples, families, American accents, murmurs of lives swirled around me, but I was shut off, unable to engage in even the most casual conversation. Arriving home exhausted in the middle of the night, I saw a lean and tall figure walking in my direction at the airport gate. It was Andy, dandy Andy, waiting for me, grinning. He picked up my bags and drove me through streets that now seemed bleak and unfamiliar, and when I got to my apartment, nothing seemed familiar to me. I glanced around, trying to orient myself, but felt only the emptiness of the place. Andy sat with me, drinking wine, listening with a frown to my decision to leave the paper, worried that I was moving too fast.

On the first day back at work I noticed a difference on the desk. Some editors shook my hand, the foreign editor gave me a friendly slap on the back, and everyone asked about my trip. But I caught the sidelong glances, the eyes that glided quickly away from my face. I had the definite impression that I had stepped into the middle of a conversation about me that I was not supposed to hear.

Later, when I went to Tim's house to have a drink with him, he lifted me in his arms and hugged me, his barrel chest a warm refuge, but after a drink or two, he said, "Everyone's talking about it, you and Elizabeth." I thought I detected disapproval. Perhaps it was his caring. I could no longer tell. I only knew that I wanted him to understand, to support and protect me. I tried to explain, but how could I explain?

He did try to understand, he did say he was on my side, but the situation pained him. It was not easy to defend me.

"She's going to tear you apart limb from limb," another friend warned me. She reminded me of past relationships she had heard me talk about and how bad I had felt then, and she reminded me, as if I needed a reminder, of the obligations I had to the paper, and my aspirations. "What happened to you before will be nothing compared to what she's going to do to you."

People are going to say you're crazy, the managing editor said when I told him I was leaving. His Irish altar-boy face was furrowed, his blue eyes widening. He was shocked at my decision, the last thing he expected, he said, playing with an empty coffee cup. We were seated in the cafeteria, midafternoon, when the lunch crowd had thinned out and we could talk without ears prying around us. I looked out the window, giving myself time, and burned my tongue on my coffee. He was rolling his wedding band, clasping and unclasping his hands.

I responded the way I do when I doubt myself, with a smile that is both a grimace and a narrowing of the eyes.

I have to do this, I said, I have to go. I couldn't begin to answer the questions I knew he had in mind, everyone's questions. I was beyond reasoning, beyond his reach. We left the table and, his hand gently at my elbow, walked down the long hallway. As we walked, I brought up Elizabeth's name lightly, inserting it between one thing or another. He noticed.

On the day I had to take the last step, to tell the editor of the paper, I crossed the length of the newsroom to his corner office and stood awkwardly at his doorway, putting on a smile, what I hoped was a smile, to win him over, to disarm him. He came around from behind his desk and invited me to take a seat on his leather couch. He sat next to me in an armchair and took sips of iced tea, his arms crossed on his chest, a finger scratching his elbow. We began with a desultory chat about Southeast Asia, his passion for it, which began when he was a war correspondent in Saigon. I was so nervous, I could feel red splotches appearing on my neck, spreading to my face, burning. He already knew why I was there, but he was letting me take my time and tried to ease my way into it. He showed me a layout of a new newspaper section he was planning, and brought over an ashtray for me, ambling across the room, his gait as slow as his southern drawl, his words making spaces between us. His mind rummaged somewhere, never exactly on point.

Finally I told him, in a burst of words I cannot remember, that I had decided to leave, that I had to go to Manila, that I had to write a book I had in my head on the Philippines. I had rehearsed this over and over, but it came out wrought and defensive. I couldn't quite look at him and picked up a cigarette to do something with my hands. He folded his arms like the buddha he was. Asia filled him with his own memories. He appraised my Manila tan, and looked around the mess of his desk for an article he recalled reading. Yes, you should go there, he said, and find out why MacArthur failed to do for the Philippines what he did for Japan. He played with my pack of cigarettes and put it down. His voice was a throaty rumble after years of cigarettes and Jameson whiskey, giving his suggestions the sonorous tone of oracle. The silence fell between us again, and lasted what seemed an hour.

"Plunge!" he said at last.

He rose from the chair and put his arm around me. "Take a year off," he said, "and come back after that. Then see."

I guessed, reading the expression in his eyes, hooded and dark, that he believed I was making the mistake of my life.

I had done it all quickly, within days of my return from Manila, shutting out, as I was prone to do, other voices, the cautionary friends, their pragmatic arguments, and my own fear that I would fail. I had nothing to show, no set of clippings, no magazine contract, and no book deal. My years in journalism had been spent almost entirely on editing desks. "You've not written much before, have you?" friends would say, pricking my balloon.

Editing had not been what I had set out to do, but from the start I had been assigned to desk jobs. Always eager to succeed and always afraid that writing would crush me, that it would only lead to grief, I had put it aside, and torn up the fragments of work that I had done over so many years. But I cannot remember a time when I did not think of myself as a writer. I believed then that writing came from the night, from someplace secret and glorious, that it came with the moon and the wind, from the simple act of breathing. I did not study it, or practice it faithfully like the scales on the piano. I was too romantic, always, for that. I did not have it sketched out, or in outlines. I did not believe it was something one talked about, discourses on style and technique, but something that came or did not come, an inspiration.

Editing had not been like that. It was a skill, at times a science. It did not create. My job had been to close the gaps in other people's stories, to find the bumps and smooth them, and I took pride in that, in the seamless paragraph, in the invisible sutures, and extracting from a reporter a clever observation, an impression that brightened the story, an interpretation that gave it depth. But editing was not writing, and I never confused the two.

I knew I would have to find the courage to write again. But I was terrified, holding on to a reef that no one else could see. I would have to start from nothing. There were many times that summer when, while I pretended to have a confidence I did not feel at all, I thought I was out of my mind. Most of my life I had battled doubts and the limits imposed on me. From the time I was a child, a diligent child, I had clung to a stubborn loneliness, saw myself standing apart, just a few steps outside whatever was around me, observing, absorbed in some other thing, never quite making the connections that seemed to make life comfortable for other people. I would devour encyclopedias and my mother's books, grown-up books — Oscar Wilde, Nabokov, García Lorca — and those lives, those words, were my reality, things that formed me. The cowboy games I played, the parties of my childhood, days in the sun with girlfriends, bicycling around the plaza, holding hands with a boyfriend, all of that was real enough but existed on the outside of me.

Elizabeth, who readily saw the things in me that were so much a part of her, too, had touched that sense of aloneness in me, had been drawn to it. I was dark and fierce and had a face of shadows and moods, a face that to her seemed ageless. I was the very thing that she wanted to avoid — chaos, intensity, a fall from grace. I was writing, passion, books, long drinks in the night. It frightened her, I thought, that I could see through her, that she couldn't lie to me, or escape me. She would say I was unlike anyone she had known, fearless, unrelenting, moving within a world that I had largely created for myself, haunted by a bottomless sorrow.

She called these things idiosyncratic. It was, she said, what she found most captivating, a way of being in the world.

The monsoon had come to Manila by the time Elizabeth moved into her apartment, after she dismantled her room at the Manila Hotel, unpinning the things on the bulletin board, her flags, her postcards and drawings. After all that time in Manila, there was little else for her but her life there, the story. She had once assumed she would return to New Delhi, but she had made Manila hers, and she wanted to stay. With one phone call to the foreign editor, she got his approval to move the paper's South Asia bureau to the Philippines. It was only a matter of packing boxes and changing addresses, and it seemed to make no difference to the Foreign Desk where she was based, New Delhi or Manila, didn't matter since she would be traveling all over Asia from one crisis to another.

She found a large, unfurnished cold-water apartment in Manila, on M. H. Del Pilar Street, on the bay side of the city, not far from the Manila Hotel. It was a tropical-style 1930s building with a rusting corrugated metal roof and streaked gray exterior walls. She moved in to the flat even before her furniture, the few pieces she had bought in India, arrived in crates from New Delhi. She had bought a bed and a rattan sofa and found in the attic of an antiques shop a swayback chair of carved wood and woven cane straw with arms almost three feet long. She got ceiling fans, a small refrigerator, a simple bed. This was her new home. It was a universe away from her house in the States, from her family linen and heirloom silver.

So much stuff, she would say, things accumulated for the sake of sheer accumulation. She owned sets of fine china and dozens of glasses and wine goblets, platters and pitchers, vases and lead-glass ashtrays, and she had left all of it in boxes, in the cellar of her house and in the dining room, stacked up in corners. With all that stuff stored away, she was living in Manila in nearly bare rooms with dark wooden floors and off-white stucco walls, cooking beans in a pot she had bought at a street market.

I measured that summer by the flights she took, the places she visited, the dust roads where she ran, the mosquitoes and bars, the broken-down jeepney on a mountain road in Davao, the smell of coconut oil in the rain. By the stories she told me on the phone, and the stories she wrote. Where did I feel her farthest, and where close: airborne five thousand feet over islands of sand so white, and thin water over coral reefs; gazing hopelessly out the window of a glass hotel into the monochrome of Taipei; surrounded by men in red bandannas in an unmapped jungle; or there, at her flat in Manila, beating cockroaches in the bathtub? I recall only slivers of her summer, off-center snapshots, and her letters—from Taiwan, from Singapore, from Sri Lanka, from thirty thousand feet in the air, flitting across the Andaman Sea to the Indian Ocean, counting the gin and tonics, dashing off postcards: elephants, strange seas, monks in saffron robes.

In Colombo, wearing her faded hunter shorts, drinking a Heineken, she wrote a note while seated on a terrace high on a hill looking over a lake. She had sat for hours, reading, watching dusk descend, the light changing on the water in the lake and the birds chasing bugs. I imagined the hill, and saw her leaning on red-clay earth, the cinders of her cigarette charring her finger-tips. I could also see her in her living room in Manila, stretched out comfortably on her Indian rug, laughing at some unintended idiom of mine. I could almost feel her breath, her hand on my knee. Her face made everything around it dim.

But she was not there in my apartment, and my nights were grim. Desolate. I would warm up a can of beans and sit at my typewriter, and when I ran out of things to write, bleary from wine, I flopped down on the sofa, turned off the floor lamp, and pulled a blanket over my legs, my arms clutching a cushion. I imagined she was done with her bedtime shower, her hair damp, matted, shining. I could smell her room in Manila, the limes in the margaritas.

On some of those nights alone, when my loneliness and doubts seemed darkest, there was nothing soothing about our phone calls. Sensing my mood, she immediately would pull back, I would feel her vanishing. Frustrated, wanting to shake her, I lashed out, prickling her stoic silence, trying to get a rise out of her. But instead, a chill fell. She had a way with silence, a mastery of it I envied, and I would flounder miserably, threaten-ing to vanish just as she did.

One day after one of those phone calls, she wrote from Anu-radhapura, in Sri Lanka, warning me that I should flee if I ever became like her. She didn't like the way she could withhold all feeling. But she could, and she knew that we would fight always over her impulse to isolate herself, and if I did the same, if I pulled back from her, then we would both be lost.

June was gone now, and I spent July giving things away. People trooped up to my apartment, picking through my closet, taking away silk blouses, winter coats, five-hundred dollar boots, and carrying out my framed *New Yorker* prints and bookcases, my collections of Agatha Christie and Nero Wolfe. And I sold my car. No one who knew me could understand why I was getting rid of everything, why it was so easy to let go of all these things. I had always found it rather easy to walk away from things, to throw them out or give them away. Even people. But I was in a hurry now, ripping off excess, shedding that skin I had lived in half my life.

Now it was a matter of counting days, waiting to take off for Manila. I imagined the roles I would play there, inventing them, seeing myself as lover, writer, journalist, wanderer, observer. There was no defined role for me in the Philippines, nothing easily explainable, nothing in evidence. And Elizabeth, I could not talk about Elizabeth. I did not then know how to begin to tell that story.

The day my house in the suburbs was sold, the house I had left so abruptly six months earlier, I was set free to go. I walked over to Tim's, half a mile in summer humidity, gulping down a cold beer.

Tim broke into one of those smiles that made me forgive him everything, his plans to see me that he would forget, dinners he didn't make. We sank into his old sofa in the fading light of the afternoon, with the shutters halfway shut, his floor fan rattling. We talked about Elizabeth, and Tim was generous, wishing me good luck and love and all those things people wish for each other, those things that friends talk about at beginnings and endings. He said he envied me my obsessions, but I didn't believe him, and we talked of little else.

Over that last month, before the departure I had scheduled for August nineteenth, a date timed to the closing on the sale of my house, which would give me the modest sum of money that would support me for a year in Manila, I would drop by to see Tim when he was in town and we would go to the backyard, where the tomato plants had grown tall and the rhododendrons were blooming. He would bring out glasses of iced coffee and bagels, cheddar, and plain crackers. He had just turned thirty, but in his Cory T-shirt and loose drawstring white pants, he seemed twenty. He saw himself flying off to crazy places and moving to Hong Kong, to live with a girlfriend there, but it was all only a fantasy. We both knew he would not go. Late in the day, Andy would bike over from his apartment and join us, bringing an onion, a can of artichokes, olives. We would sit in the backyard, with Tim's jazz tapes playing, and drink rum straight up. Right around dusk, bloated and drowsy, Tim would light up the grill and put on a chicken, and the dark would settle over the three of us.

Tim was gone much of the time, on assignment in Washington. His house was half empty, so Andy moved in and took up the second floor, where I used to stay. I broke my lease on my apartment and friends helped me pack my remaining things into a truck and haul the load to Tim's, where I stored boxes that over the years I would forget—a stereo player, family pictures, kitchen bowls. We jammed my rust-colored sofa against the boarded-up fireplace on the ground floor, laid my rugs in the living room, and stashed away the rest of my things in the basement. The place was transformed suddenly, a mishmash of Tim's hand-me-downs and my terra cotta colors, a palette of burnt siennas.

The last weeks were a blur. I drank with friends, had going-away parties at restaurants, consumed bottles of white wine, countless rounds of beer. I made arrangements at my bank, closed accounts, changed addresses. I was planning to go away only for a year, and the paper had given me a leave of absence, but I was putting everything in order, performing last rites.

One day the mail brought me Elizabeth's Manila Blues volume 3 — "a last blast from a tortured brain." She said she dreamed of my anger and my moods and awoke feeling lonely, wondering how solitary she might have been if she had never met me. She no longer brooded the way she had months earlier, during our first days together when I visited Manila, when she was uncertain about us and afraid of what our relationship would do to her life. Now there was little visible trace of the deep upheaval she had felt then, but I believed there was uncertainty still, a fear perhaps of a life new to her. When she was not traveling, she meandered around the streets of Manila, fending off beggars, buying cigarettes and Hershey's Kisses, going to the turo-turo for a bite of dinner, maybe rice noodles or crispy chicken, in the rain. It was the start of the rainy season and she felt so lonely, she said, she could feel the emptiness on her skin.

On my last day at work they brought me a cake and champagne. Everyone stood around, not quite knowing what to say. There were toasts, bloated words. Finally everyone dispersed, and banging closed the drawers of my desk, emptying them of me, and logging off the computer terminal, I rolled off my chair and glanced around one last time at our map of the world and the rubber chicken hanging from the ceiling over the managing editor's desk. I took down my postcards and notes, and skipped out, running down the stairs, through the beveled front doors.

Two days later, on the morning of my departure, Tim stood with me on the stoop. He was on his way back to Washington on a new assignment and was wearing his single business suit, dark blue, with an old wrinkled tie. After embracing me, crushing me against him, he walked off. His shoulders sagged, his head drooped. I watched him, missing him already.

Andy took me to the airport. We sat in a cocktail lounge, drinking beer, tearing at wet napkins, watching the clock, not saying much. Then it was time to go. I felt a sudden void, and I stood on my toes to kiss his cheek, brushing his hair as he bent down to hold me. Turning away from him, I picked up my bags and went through the gate.

Thirty thousand feet over the South China Sea, Elizabeth was at that moment flying south to Manila from Taiwan, heading home to greet me. *There is a typhoon moving west, just now, toward China,* she scribbled. *It has rained a lot lately. That much is true. Welcome to Manila.*

PART II

5

WHEN I LOOK back to that August in Manila, I must
begin with the rain. It came in gulps, torrents, slashing
across the world, drowning it. The sky, a crisscross of flashes,
lightning snapping, became a vast black sea, exploding. Palm
trees lashed by high winds from the south bowed to the ground,
and people caught in a tempest of wind and rain, light and thun-
der, were washed away, helpless. The afternoon became night
suddenly and the city, a city of ten million lights, became a phan-
tasm, ghostly.

Elizabeth and I would watch it come from the casement windows of the apartment, our candles burning and the wind hissing
through the cracks, the lightning close enough to touch, but we
had no fear, no sense of disaster. We felt pure, and the rain, the
fury in the sky, seemed a miracle, an omen.

This time, on the day of my arrival, August 21, 1986, Elizabeth was waiting for me at the airport. She was scanning the
crowd. But naturally, I saw her first. Then she caught my eye,
gave me a palms-up wave, a little salute, and moved toward me
without any apparent rush. She was not one to come running
with open arms. But she had that smile of wonder, a slight swing

to her stride and a cocky tilt to her head, looking neither directly at me nor away but focused all the same. She reached around me to stroke my hair, light and casual, as if anything could be casual about this. And picking up a piece of luggage, she led the way out of the terminal.

The waiting car was the same spic-and-span Crown Victoria with the bleached white slipcovers that had, in the spring, taken me to the Manila Hotel the first time. Rolly was again at the wheel, like he was that day in March, but now he was flushed with the excitement of having me back in town. In the back seat, Elizabeth and I fell into our public roles, awkward, nervous, superficial. We kept interrupting each other with simple chatter, as if we were old but distant friends catching up. How was your flight? What's going on in Manila? How's the apartment?

She was good at tamping down emotion, but I could sense her loneliness and her toughness, the marks of those months from May to August of solitary living. With me there, our proximity obliterating all that, her voice took on a light, cheerful note and her face was lit up. Uneasy, I kept looking away, out the window, not at Manila, because Manila was no longer new to me, but to avoid her eyes, to find a proper distance, to avoid being drawn in too quickly by the perfume that came from her. But then I glanced over and was startled again that she was so oddly beautiful, that she was there.

We had a year, or perhaps only weeks, months, or an eternity. We did not know how much time we had, how much time we would last together, because nothing about us had come conventionally, arranged, foreseen, with preambles and assurances. In the back of the car with her, having left a life behind me, I was unsure of myself. I played with my hair, clutched a magazine, and noticing my anxiety, she reached out and touched my hand. With that single gesture she was reassuring me and herself, and when we were finally alone in her apartment, relaxed on her white rattan sofa, I touched her cheek and felt the elation that ran through her.

She took a week off from work to help me get settled in the vacant apartment I rented on the same floor as hers. By the time I arrived, she had bought me a table lamp, handmade in Mindanao, with a glazed wooden base in deep rose and plum and a wide cloth shade stained burgundy. She had set it up on a plain table by a window, where I would sit for hours and write. She had big hopes for me and my writing and brought me stacks of copy paper, pens and clips, dictionaries, maps. I took the apartment not because I wanted to have a separate home, but because Elizabeth did. She said she wanted her own place, her own things, wanted to find her own way. For a few weeks, I pretended to live in my apartment, but I never slept there. My clothes hung in her apartment.

Days and nights fused and everything around us became ours: the restaurants and cafés, the foul streets, the morning fog on the bay, and the moments when, sinking into that city so strange and intimate, we lost all fear. Mornings came after nights when geckos crawled up the walls and we lay in our bed listening to the preludes and canons that had become the backdrop to our silences. There was nothing that came before those nights, before those hours, hours that for me transcended years, anguish and ache, insatiable longing. Tears that had accumulated in me in the years that came before her would burst out suddenly, and I would drift into a dreamless sleep, her arm around me. I would wake up to the sprinkling of her shower, the sun already above the horizon. Through the bedroom window, you could see the coconut palms in the Malate plaza and overhear, even with the window shut and the ceiling fan turning, the cranking of buses and jeepneys on the street below.

We ate out almost every night, usually at Café Adriatico, under the Cinzano umbrellas, as we had the first night I spent in Manila in the spring and the first night of my return in August. That evening in August the lights went out, leaving the city dark, and we, oblivious to all, kept talking and drinking and picking at the calamari. Our evenings at Adriatico were a kind of refuge, a Parisian scene, with garlic shrimp on our plates or fondue burning, Bordeaux and the chant of the flower vendors, and running home careless in a thunderstorm.

Other nights we had dinner at the Weinstube, a German bistro nearby. As we walked down the tawdry blocks to get there, on torn-up sidewalks crawling with roaches and past gutters stinking of garbage, Elizabeth, loping half a dozen steps ahead of me, laughed as she stepped on the bugs and skipped like a kid over sidewalk cracks. The Weinstube had vacuumed carpets and white linen tablecloths, slithering waitresses, and a piano player. It was the kind of whispery place where expats began their days of drinking in midafternoon. The owner, a willowy Filipina in a tight madam dress and with sharp red fingernails, would slide

up the piano stool around midnight and take requests, which invariably ran to "As Time Goes By" and "My Funny Valentine,"
songs wafting over rapt guests in a 1940s setting of shimmering
table candles and snifters of Rémy Martin and Courvoisier.

We walked everywhere those first months—to the San An-
dres market down a slummy street and bought potatoes and
plantains, pineapples, mangoes and papaya, and the rare piece
of fresh fish that had not rotted lying out in open, unrefrigerated
stalls covered with flies. We found cloth napkins, place mats, iron
pans, inexpensive household stuff, all spread out on straw mats
at the market. We felt happily invisible among the barrio people,
the housemaids who shopped for the expats, and the farmers,
shirtless men in flip-flops smoking pungent local cigarettes. We
bought clay pots for cooking, wooden bowls, and big fat candles
to set on Elizabeth's steamer trunk. Slowly we made a home.

By now I had moved in entirely to her apartment and left
mine partly furnished but unoccupied. Her apartment got more
light than mine, with casement windows on three sides. The
building, dating back to the American colonial era, had seen
much better days. The exterior had gone from art deco pas-
tels to a dirty gray. The ground floor flooded, and the stairwell
had dead potted plants and a chipped plaster statue of the Child
Christ. The building had its history. Alex the landlord, a short,
stocky Filipino who brought in young girls from the provinces
to work as housekeepers, sweepers, and laundrywomen, would
come to our door on one pretext or another. His eyes roamed
around, checking the furniture, the rugs, the hangings on the
living room walls, and kept us standing politely while he reeled

off stories about the Japanese and American soldiers who fought hand to hand in those rooms during World War II. He was a vivid storyteller, had the typical Filipino knack for drama, painting for us scenes of war and bloodshed and bodies spattering on those walls. The ghosts of the soldiers cursed the place, he said in a sinister whisper, and caused earthquakes.

And, of course, MacArthur had once stayed there. MacArthur had stayed everywhere.

From our second floor we had only a side view of the bay, but the city of beggars and restless commerce lay beneath the wide double windows of our living room. We kept the venetian blinds drawn at night, shutting out the orange and red tiled sex motel across the street, where couples snuck in behind tinted windows, their cars disappearing inside. On the other side we looked over the roof of a *lechon manok* restaurant, the most popular on Roxas Boulevard. On days when the wind came from a certain direction, the stench of fumes from the restaurant's exhaust pipes seeped into our flat, stinking up the place; the trash from the restaurant's kitchen sat uncollected for weeks near the entrance to our building, spilling out on the street, garbage piles torn up by dogs and rats.

We had three large rooms, a gloomy, sunless kitchen with an old gas stove and linoleum counters, and a maid's room with a bunk bed and a shower. The rooms had chocolate-brown floors, wax-shined wooden planks, high ceilings, and whitewashed rough stucco walls. It was a flat of onetime elegance, a place of cobwebs in the corners and food smells. Elizabeth's things — rice baskets, a couple of primitive Malay spears, a lopsided wicker sideboard, a pair of Rajasthani chairs, assorted rugs, and the long-armed chair called a butaca — defined the apartment, set a spare, monastic tone.

These rooms had nothing of our past. In time they became entirely our own, with our things, which we would carry with us from place to place over the years.

We talked endlessly in those rooms. Elizabeth, who had buried so much for so long, unfolded her life slowly, sometimes in streams of words, as if she had not really spoken for ten years, as if she had long ago dropped out of ordinary life. She called her twenties a time of anomie, when she cut herself off from the things that had once moved her — books, music, art, and writing. "I don't read, I don't listen to music," she had said when I first met her, and I thought then that it was some sort of sophomoric cynicism, a juvenile affectation.

She had once bought a small farm and had spent her weekends dismantling the old farmhouse plank by plank. She had planted a garden and a row of fruit trees. For a time she believed she would remake it into the peaceful, private place she thought she needed. But it was never finished. Often she warned me about voices that were loud and clear in her head, and her belief then that life was bare and frail, to be lived alone, a point that came between us again and again. When I would try to smash through that, she would balk, retreating to some place in her head where I could not follow. Her detachment at times confounded me. She liked to say she was a clam, deep in a shell. She didn't want to stick out and expose the layers underneath. Her distant manner was studied, learned since childhood, I supposed, and by now it came naturally, shading the insecurities that I saw sometimes gnawing at her. Buttoned down, impervious at times, she was the very picture of upper-class Protestant girls groomed to a life in which emotions were meant to be disguised and pushed down. That surface, a carapace I used to call it, had little to do with the other Elizabeth, passionate and intense to the core.

But there were things I did not talk about, things she wanted to know, about broken loves and long parts of my life I left vague. Family, relationships, old anger. Scars had grown over some wounds — a father who drank too much and carried on with too many women, a devastated mother, a family torn apart — and I refused to rip them open again. I had buried all that so far down, had spent years pouring earth over those memories, I was not going to dredge them up. But it wasn't the family wounds I avoided most. Broken relationships were best forgotten, I thought, best left to wither away.

"I hate it when you do that," she said every time I clammed up, reversing our usual roles. "You go up to your balcony, looking down from up there, distant. I can't reach you there."

Sometimes I fell into a dead stare, my face turned away from hers. While she was careful, probing what she knew were my wounds, I was intractable with her, insisting to know it all. Different as we were, we were fighting each other over the same things. We had lived through these things in our phone calls and letters, but without distance to protect us, and isolated in this place, there was no escape. It seemed to me that our relationship broke all patterns, and I marveled at its force, and sometimes I was frightened.

Passion comes rarely, and when it comes, it can be like a sei-
zure, uprooting everything, consuming and transforming, taking possession, and at the same time, freeing spirit and flesh. It
brings with it all that we are and have been, incalculable joy and
unmeasurable wreckage. Ours was that, all of that. I saw it even
then. My depression, her fears; my dreams for her, her belief in
me; my hunger for her, her need of me.

One afternoon, the day I found out I was not getting a writing fellowship I had worked on for months, I paced up and down
the apartment, flaying myself, drinking beer after beer. When
she came in she took a look at my face, and she braced for the
bout she knew would follow. She put a hand on my back, wanting to comfort me, but I froze at her touch and walked away. I
grabbed pages of my writing in my fist, throwing them around
the room. She sat down, helpless, her face caught in a vise, narrowing, beaked. I had never known a face that could change quite
like that, neither angry nor sad, but implacable. She was rigid,
jaws clenched, lips locked. Her composure was maddening. It
set us apart. I turned on her with fury, hoping my anger would
draw her out. It was a cycle we would repeat time and again.

For me, the bleakness swallowed everything. In those black
holes I fell into, residues of my childhood, when the anger turned
inside me, crowding out anything light, I felt in the grip of fail-
ure. Perhaps I was reliving my drunken father's belligerence or
my brave mother's emotional subjugation. I saw no future for
me, for Elizabeth and me together. I saw nothing but abandonment and rejection. She was holding something back from me, I
suspected. In time she would leave me.

Elizabeth would listen to the storm raging in me. It horrified and ripped her. "This is the one thing that will destroy us," she said, exasperated. She could not stand to watch me tear myself apart, she said again and again. She could not stand to hear the bitterness in my voice, lacerations I intended for myself but that pierced her, too. That night she left her chair and came over to me, grabbed me and pushed me against the wall and held me in her arms, and while I seemed to recover quickly, she was left drained.

I didn't understand then that my moods were harder on her than they were on me.

There were times when she left me alone, unable to stand by while I ranted that she was impervious and unfeeling. She would walk out without a word and be gone for hours. On her birthday, when she had been caught up in her work and I was frustrated, unable to write, she slipped away, and thought about the insults I had hurled at her.

"You've decided that I am horrid, cold, and calculating," she told me later. "Why the hell do you live with me then?"

These fights, with their familiar feints and skin pricks, seemed to blow over in hours or days, and we would once again pick up where we had left off, our intimacy nearly intact.

My first letter from Manila was to Tim, a sketch of the place, a place he had known, but now through my eyes, in my time. A day after he got my letter, he called to tell me he loved it, that I must write just like that. Was he serious? For a moment I believed him, and went back to the typewriter. I had set up my table and bookshelves in a large room Elizabeth had made into her office. It had a ceiling fan, her desk, which she brought from India, and her bookcases. She had the window view. I had the windowless end of the room. Settled there with the books I had bought in a storefront nearby and Elizabeth's Philippine flag, which she had nailed to a wall, I wrote for hours, tearing up page after page, tossing crumpled pages around the room, my back aching from sitting on a straight-backed chair. But I was also determined, driven, teaching myself, trying to see.

The rains came, not sporadically but constantly, day after day, flooding the city for weeks. The scene that became commonplace for me: poor souls carrying bundles on their heads, wading in sodden rivers that just hours before had been their streets. By six in the morning Elizabeth was at work, making phone calls, running out to cover a demonstration, setting up interviews at the presidential palace, at Camp Aguinaldo, at the American embassy, the three power centers of the capital. Coming home late, covered in sweat and mud, she would plop down at her typewriter, cursing the hours stalled in traffic, the taxi drivers, the monsoon, the president, the ambassador.

There was nothing simple about Manila.

With the typhoons and the drownings at sea and all the disasters that accompanied the season came the rumors of a coup. Everyone knew that military factions were plotting to take power from Cory Aquino, and had been doing so since the day she became president in February 1986. By autumn, only seven months into her presidency, there was a palpable edginess about the city. People jumped when the lights went out and when army trucks rolled down Roxas Boulevard. We couldn't get a drink at the Lobby Lounge or drop by the Peninsula Hotel coffee shop without hearing the latest gossip, whispers, asides.

We ran from rumor to rumor, trying to make sense out of fantasy, conspiracies printed as fact in the local papers, speculation from columnists and generals and Cory's Harvard-smooth presidential aides. Some days I stayed behind in the apartment, working on an outline of a book I wanted to write, a story of the Philippines at that special crossroads in its history, after twenty years of Marcos, the flavor and scenes and characters caught up in that moment. I would sit bent over the typewriter, in the chair with the hard seat and the shaky back, staring blankly at the walls, making lists of books I had to read, research I had to do, and people I had to interview.

I wandered around the apartment, feeling caged at times, turning up the music, flipping through magazines, watching Gina, our maid, an eighteen-year-old from Tarlac province who came in to do laundry and wax the floors. With her bare feet she rubbed a dry coconut husk on the floorboards, back and forth, a sort of dance. I would watch the lavanderas—the laundry-women—on the roof over the garage, scrubbing the laundry by hand with coarse bars of soap and dipping it in tin tubs, and eating their lunch on their haunches, giggling.

The sight of them took me back to my childhood, when I was nine and my family lived among lavanderas and farmers on an unpaved road in a town in eastern Puerto Rico where my father was doing his residency at the municipal hospital, delivering poor women's babies, making middle-of-the-night house calls. We would be there two years, the length of time the government

demanded of my father for giving him a grant to study medicine. The first few months we lived in a wooden house, set up
on stilts, with a cold-water shower behind the kitchen. Later we
moved up the road to a cinderblock house painted bright pink,
with a carport and an unfenced backyard with a wire chicken
coop and guava and tamarind trees. The maid came early to
feed the chickens and wash our clothes in tin tubs in the yard.
She mopped our floors and fixed our meals and filled the house
with the smell of garlic and onions. In the afternoons, before
my mother got home from her work at the superior court in San
Juan, I would get out of my starched Catholic school uniform,
take a shower, and run out to the vacant field across from the
house to play baseball with the neighborhood boys, the whacks
of our bats the loudest sounds at sundown.

Gina's face and the lavanderas on the roof brought that back
to me and reminded me of the pages I had written for myself,
island memories, loose sheets of descriptions I had left incom-
plete. Far into the afternoon I would go back to my butaca,
the long-armed chair, with a beer can dripping wet on the side
table, a book in my hands. The living room was in shadows.
Gina would come in with a basket of laundry and, too shy to say
anything to me, would pad to the maid's room to do the iron-
ing. Around sundown, when there was no sunlight left and I was
still in the Filipino chair, a leg hanging over its long wooden
arm, the book propped in my hand, not many pages past where
I had started hours earlier, she would emerge, her face glisten-
ing from the hot iron, carrying our clothes, shirts flowing on
hangers, buttoned up and hung the way Elizabeth had taught

her. With another hand she carried an armful of towels, sheets, underwear — everything fluffed and folded in squares and smelling of sunshine.

Days would go by like that, without my writing a single sentence. Days of walks around the block, getting cigarettes, coconut ice cream, newspapers. Days around the pool at the Manila Hotel, days at the Lobby Lounge in my khaki jacket, meeting socialites and newspaper editors, politicians and militants. I was always taking notes, scribbles that later made little sense to me, unintelligible handwriting, half sentences, unfinished quotes. Interviews lasted hours, over lunch and into the afternoon *merienda,* Manila's teatime, and by the time they were over I would feel numb, coming out of the interviews into the glaring sun.

I stored it all away in some fashion: The Filipina-Chinese heiress, extravagantly chic and rapaciously greedy, who had calculated when she would be married and to whom, the idea being to leave the country, consumed one entire afternoon over lunch at Eva's Garden. How she laughed at gullible Filipinos and their People Power Revolution, saying the country needed rivers of blood, her fingernails like pincers as she raised a bite of shrimp to her fuchsia mouth.

Another day, in the dusty dimness of a room above a shabby bookshop in Ermita, I listened to the laments of a famous novelist, darling of the foreign press. He was bald and chubby like a monk, a leftist radical from the old Marcos days who had already given up on Cory, his last hope. Like other leftists who had thrown themselves into Cory's campaign, he was already disappointed in her slow approach to economic and military reforms.

They all had expected centuries of history to change overnight when she was sworn in. Worse, Cory had ignored his advice, the packs of reform proposals he had labored over and presented to her. Look, he said, sighing with resignation and pointing at a thick pile of reports, at all the work he had put into it!

One evening, in the swelter of a cocktail party at a downtown apartment of heavy foam-filled cushions covered in loud ruby colors, I met a celebrated human rights lawyer, a University of Manila professor with a Yale degree. With wild hair and her eyes bulging with excitement, she talked with heartfelt admiration about civil society in Chile, where she had been an international election observer, and described with equal amounts of horror and self-satisfaction her work crisscrossing the Philippine islands, cataloging massacres and monitoring election abuses. Smart as a whip and sharp-tongued, she could mount an impressive diatribe against the Filipino military, yet could just as easily turn around and hug the most notorious military rogue at the party.

Manila then seemed to me a universe away from America. I was always startled to see President Reagan or any footage from the United States on the TV news in Manila. The streets and cars I saw in the American news sparkled, the buildings shimmered. The politics in Washington seemed bland and rigidly civilized. Everyone looked blond, groomed, and smug. We subscribed to the *International Herald Tribune* and I waited for it every afternoon, then read every word of it. The Wall Street boom, Trump, Gorbachev, Nancy Reagan and Raisa Gorbachev photographed together in the White House: an orderly world, another planet.

At that time, the last months of 1986, there were at least two dozen people writing books about the Philippines. Big books on the fall of Marcos, on hidden wealth, on Imelda, on the history of the country. Every journalist who had ever set foot in the place was writing something, and the ideas in my head seemed odd and abstract measured against theirs and their familiarity with the country. They were everywhere, at the tables by the pool at the Manila Hotel, mooching drinks; at parties with Cory's confidantes; at little dinners in Ermita penthouses, getting dizzy on piña coladas and gorging on stir-fry Mongolian beef and oxtail kare-kare.

It took me no time at all to rein in the invitations, to know the names, the twisted connections, and every morning, I would scour the local papers, a half dozen of them, for the latest scandal. Manila had little else but scandal, corruption, sex, and gossip. On the cocktail circuit, and in the air-conditioned offices in the business district of Makati, where the political insiders courted the foreign press, I could be earnest, a veteran of the place. I clipped the papers and made files, a habit I had from newspapering, of putting things in order.

I was making a niche for my writing, but the truth was not that at all. I was getting caught in the quagmire of Manila, the press circles and political intrigue, avoiding the drudgery of writing and the long, solitary hours at the typewriter.

Elizabeth had little patience for my impatience.

"It takes time," she kept saying. She had her rules about these things, a steel will, discipline, method, and trying to encourage me, she would say, "All those things other people are writing, what they think, what they say, where they go, have nothing to do with you, with your work."

She had high dreams for me, and notions of writing that were even more idealized than mine were in those years. She believed writers worked in solitude, removed from the world outside, from money, fame, and glamour. She imagined taking herself away to a ramshackle farm or a deserted southern shore, marking her days by the shift of the wind, the flight patterns of geese.

I rented my vacant apartment down the hall to a bouncy young field producer for the American networks, and soon she was having the walls painted pink, the furniture reupholstered in flowery fabrics, and chintz draperies hung on the casement windows. She was a charmer, Kay was, with a freckled pudgy face, lank dark brown hair, and moist caramel eyes.

The first time we met she suggested a restaurant in Makati, a fancy place with the best local food in the city, where the dishes came in platters—krispy pata, crabs boiled in coconut juice. Elizabeth had already met her and had put her off. But I wanted to meet her, had heard talk about her, and Elizabeth came along to the lunch because I insisted.

Her voice buttery, Kay said she had heard so much about me. Over dinner, she wooed us both with flattery, raving about Elizabeth's writing and my quick grasp of the political scene. She wrapped herself around us, squeezing my arm, nodding attentively at every utterance, and she flooded us with inside gossip. Living down the hall from us, she was in our life before we knew it. She was always in trouble and she was always in crisis. One day she was being fired, another day she was running out of money, on yet another day she had heard people gossiping about her. She would make herself at home in our apartment, plopping down on the floor, her skirt riding up her thighs, and her hand pulling at strands of her hair. We listened to whatever she rattled on about and brought out apples and Brie and wine, taking her seriously. It was a foolish thing, because she didn't listen to advice. The next day, the crisis of the moment would pass and she would stay in bed late, tangled in thick covers, calling up her sources, hounding them, and at the same time talking to us while a skinny Filipina she found somewhere gave her a massage, rubbing oil over Kay's naked body.

Elizabeth didn't take to people as easily as I did, always keeping her distance for a long time. Kay was smart, shrewd, and manipulative when she went after someone, and Elizabeth didn't trust her. But she was not immune, playing big sister to Kay's helpless wastrel, sitting her down for lectures on demeanor, rewriting her memos to her bosses. Kay loved her. To me she would say, "You have a darkness in you," adding, "Elizabeth is the only one among us who is pure." I would nod, thinking she was saying what she thought I believed. I did!

Other people came around our apartment from time to time. There were photographers and TV crews we knew from our Sundays by the pool who would come to our door uninvited. Elizabeth and I would sit far apart, not looking at each other, keeping ourselves from revealing any intimacy. But they knew. I could see in their curious glances the questions they didn't dare ask: What was I doing there exactly, how did I support myself, how could we get away with this in Manila?

One night Camilla came over, tall and slender, smoking Marlboro reds, hipless in jeans, her photographer's bag stuffed with lenses and rolls of film. She was a Brit, educated in boarding schools, and had the rich European girl's throwaway beauty — long legs, a model's cheekbones. Elizabeth had fallen in with her the day they met at a press conference. Camilla was one of those few people whom Elizabeth spotted from time to time and claimed as her own. She was the only person Elizabeth had mentioned to me in letters and phone calls during our time apart over the summer, and the only photographer whose company she enjoyed. Together they had gone up rough roads on horses and had drunk rum with the communist rebels and survived a jeepney crash and the leers of the troops in hillside stations. Camilla had come from Hong Kong to do some freelancing in the Philippines.

The night she came over to pick up Elizabeth for dinner, she said she was thinking of moving to Manila and taking a house in a compound of houses not far from us. Looking around at Elizabeth's things, she was also taking me in. I felt uneasy, guessing that she had not figured out what I was to Elizabeth. Without any makeup, her hair loose around her thin shoulders, she was plain but striking at the same time. She was there a few minutes and then they were gone to dinner, and the next time I saw her, a few days later, at a party inaugurating the foreign press club's headquarters, she was wearing dangling earrings and rouge, and a mid-thigh black dress that made deep curves of her narrow hips, and she had her manicured hand on Nick's shoulder, Nick, who was dazzling in white linen, copper-haired and bronzed.

In the tricky month of November, when the typhoon season draws down and the taxi drivers predict that the rains are over just as a rainstorm breaks out, we heard the coup would come any day. We would sit around the Manila Hotel, waiting, drinking in the Lobby Lounge, skimming the wire stories ripped off the CBS and NBC offices upstairs. Midnight or two in the morning, the phone would ring at home, and a voice would whisper, "It's tonight." Reporters scattered around town, to the army headquarters at Camp Aguinaldo, to Malacañang Palace, where the sandbags were piled at the gates. Barricades were going up around Cory's house, a modest home secluded in a block down the street from her offices in an annex at the palace. On the short wave we heard about the troops moving from the north, armored tanks moving from the south; troops moving to secure the perimeter, the government's TV and radio stations, and the airport.

The city was muffled. Streets empty of cars, lights out. At three in the morning, or later, Rolly, our constant driver, was taking us around the city. We were looking for troops, for tanks and men in camouflage taking up positions, anything to suggest that a coup was in process. We found nothing but military checkpoints. Rolly, who was no hero at times like these, stuttered in Tagalog as he handed over his documents at checkpoints, but Elizabeth swayed the guards, dangling her foreign press credentials and flashing her American smile. Around town there were hundreds of international correspondents and photographers. Dozens had flown in from Beijing, Tokyo, San Francisco, New York, Rome, anticipating another revolt, a little bang-bang, maybe the fall of Cory Aquino.

Nothing really happened. No one could actually report that troops moved, any troops. No one saw anything; no shots were ever fired. But Cory Aquino, identifying her enemies, immediately fired the defense minister, the same defense minister who had backed her against Marcos, and put him under house arrest. His "boys," the colonels and lieutenants who had banded around him to force Marcos out, were put under arrest in the barracks.

The aftermath of the coup that was or was not a coup left us all frazzled, troops without a war, sitting around the hotel lobby figuring out the next move. I had made myself part of the press corps, insinuated myself into it. Elizabeth had resisted at first, did not want to be seen with me at her side everywhere, but eventually the work became an extension of our private life, rounds of high agitation, vigils on rooftops, mesmerizing tales told in mansions draped in jacarandas.

Christmas comes early in Manila. The stores, warding off the evils of the rainy season and desperate for the burst of spending of the holidays, hang their twinkling lights early in November and set up their manger scenes and imported Christmas trees wrapped in angel hair. Plastic Santas glow red and white, night and day, on display windows. The temperature is ninety degrees, but shopping malls turn up their scratchy tapes of "White Christmas" and grocery stores stockpile eggnog and fruitcakes, cranberry jellies, hams and turkeys. By mid-December, offices close early and the government ceases to function. Churches toll their bells, barrios have their fiestas, and religious processions fill the streets. There's a run on fireworks, and the hotels feature evenings of choral music, with children from orphanages, from the slums and parochial schools, singing out, eyes to the sky, with such wispy voices that tears come to your eyes.

On our first Christmas in Manila we went to Boracay, a sand island in the central Philippines, a holiday haven then still rural, without paved roads, without electricity, but already discovered, its name printed on beach towels and T-shirts. We left Manila early on Christmas Day, after opening the gifts we had placed under our tree, a potted ficus Elizabeth had strung with white lights and trimmed with handmade Filipino ornaments she'd bought in the street markets: small straw birds, miniature brooms, peasant hats.

Our four-seat plane to Boracay wobbled above the clouds the two hours of the flight south and sputtered to a landing on a grassy field bordered by coconut trees. We braked at a thatched shed, where we waited with the roosting chickens for a motored tricycle to take us to the dock, a shack where tourists bought tickets to cross by boat to Boracay. There was in this crossing of water, a roiling over slapping waves, a sense of infinite space, a panoramic sea. Soon we were within sight of sand and palms, the sand chalk white, and against it an awning of palm fronds, trunks bent in the wind.

We had no hotel reservations, and Christmas was Boracay's high season. Dragging our duffels, we wandered up and down a boardwalk, looking for a vacancy. Just when we were about to give up we found Casa del Pilar, half a dozen cottages standing on concrete blocks and making a semicircle around a rustic restaurant. Our room had two wooden cots, foam mattresses, and a toilet flushed by dumping a bucket of water into it. We had a porch, and at sundown the houseboys came by with torchlights.

In the days we spent there, days that began with the sunrise, we got around to the village a mile beyond, a cluster of taverns, cheap motels, and vendor stalls. We bought drawstring shorts made of flour sacks, beach towels, and straw hats, and slogged on burning sand back across the island, slapping at sand flies in the air. Elizabeth went windsurfing and fell laughing into the water, and she took out a catamaran and disappeared in the horizon while I lay peering into the sun, trying to spot her. For a long time there was nothing out there, and just as I was beginning to panic, I saw her, a tiny figure in that distance. She came ashore pulling the boat by a rope. I ran up to her, all worry, but she had on her happy shark smile, wide-mouthed, all teeth, the look she must have had the day when she was a kid who, wanting to run away from home, had taken a dinghy out into a storm.

Late in the afternoons we would walk to the far point of Boracay. We were wanderers, tourists, picking up shells along the way, our backs to the sun, our skin gritty and broiled. At sundown the houseboys lit the garden torches, and we read and drank gin and tonics on our porch, bare feet on the rail. Darkness fell quickly and in our room a candle burned, and we would go to sleep hot and sweaty to the beat of maracas and drums and the stomping of couples dancing in the nightclub next door.

On our final night, the last of five, we walked over to a restaurant by the water, a long way from our cottage, close to the village. There were sand floors and bare tables and dogs licking our toes, and the smell of barbecue and coal fires. On the way back we came on a deserted piece of beach and lay down on the sand and she named for me all the stars and the constellations, tracing in the air the shape of the Big Dipper and the archer and the bear. After a little while we dusted our shorts off and walked to our place in the dark, which was not like the dark of night anywhere else.

It was a time, our first year together in Manila, when our lives, our days and nights, everything about us, seemed braided. Twists and strands that even now I cannot possibly separate. It was New Year's Day, 1987, and we were lying by the Manila Hotel pool, my skin deeply tanned from Boracay, my hair darkened by the sun, in feathery curls, and already, by noon, we were into our second or third beers, surrounded by friends, familiar faces, the regulars. Everyone was out that day.

Elizabeth did laps in the pool, her striped pink and white tank suit slick on her skin, revealing ribs, flat stomach. She moved like seaweed in the water, her freckled shoulders rising, churning, and when she came out of the pool, toweling her hair, she squeezed in next to me and Nick. He brushed his mustache on her cheek, a brotherly kiss, and challenged her to a game of tennis. Nothing she would like better, beating him on the court, and others came around, Nick's drinking mates, leathery faces you saw here and there, all over the Far East.

No scuttling clouds this day, not a trace of smog. There was a carefree informality, the camaraderie of people thrown together, and we drank and talked all afternoon. I thought I would never leave Manila, that none of us could.

We had no routine, except the morning coffee that Elizabeth

brewed in an old iron pot, standing in the kitchen waiting for the water to boil and then pouring it through the nozzle, one cup at a time. Her days had an unpredictable rhythm. She was not bound to an office clock or a set number of stories. With the slow pace of a new year, she would take a day or two to write a long piece for the front page, organizing her notes, starting and restarting her lead, writing postcards to the office, breaking away for a beer on the couch with me. On other days she was out the door early, going on interviews, arranging for trips to the provinces, doing what reporters do.

My days had no clear schedule, no hour when I began work and when I finished, no deadlines except those I imposed on myself, making believe that something would come out of these hours bowed at my desk, over my typewriter keys, envisioning lines and lines of prose, and imagining on those days when the writing came swiftly that it would always be like this.

Elizabeth, who in our early months together had fought to keep her life distinct from mine, close but separate, now would come into our apartment after a day out and call my name the second she opened the door. She always surprised me doing this, calling my name as if she had just returned from a long trip. Dumping her shoulder bag on the floor, she would wash the grime off her face, and, grabbing a beer, talking all the while, she would give me the details of her day: the places she visited, the people she met. An interview with the American ambassador one day, a schoolteacher the next, and one day, an audience with President Aquino. For that one, Elizabeth put on a long skirt, a silk blouse, and a string of pearls and arrived at Malacañang

Palace in a chauffeured black Mercedes, because she wanted to impress and because the palace did not allow taxicabs inside the grounds, where Cory had her office.

On any day, no matter how tired she was, she would put aside whatever she had to do and pick up the pages I had written that day and would listen to everything I was saying. We talked for hours, sometimes looped side by side on the sofa, sometimes stretched out on the carpet. Then the telephone would ring and she had to go off to her desk and start writing a story, but pulling me to her, her hand grazing the nape of my neck, she would wait a minute longer.

I took up tennis that spring, played early in the morning three times a week with Leo, the Manila Hotel pro. He hand-lobbed balls over the net again and again, making me run from one end to another. I missed every time. Old Leo had the patience of a saint, with sweat dripping down his big round face, down the rolls of fat around his neck and collar. He would yell at me, "Move your feet, move your feet," just when I thought I was racing across the court. My elbow would not bend easily, my legs were not strong enough, my feet slow. But he kept at me. He spread his bulging arms around me, his hand squashing my bones as he tried to teach me how to hold the racket, how to twist and twirl. I practiced at home, swinging my Prince Pro against the air, tossing a ball up to the ceiling and watching it plop on the floor nowhere near my racket. I was artless, I knew, playing tennis the way I had played baseball when I was a kid. I would feel again that thrill of childhood, when I blazed around town in roller skates, or hit a home run, or leaped down the plaza stairs on my bike. Leo kept pushing me, "leetle by leetle." Occasionally, not often, Elizabeth dropped by the courts, clapping when I hit the ball back and over, cheering me on.

She made me think I could do just about anything. She said I had the mind and the heart, that I was bold and daring. A mountain, she called me sometimes. It was an image she fashioned for me, and I allowed myself to believe it. I still had my moods, when I crashed to the bottom. But less often, and I was not despairing. I had a resolve, and if things took longer for me, if sometimes I blocked myself, I would in the end find the way. I had believed that since childhood, had lived it. But somehow, here, it was coming true. She knew the stubborn streak I had: how I flew thirteen thousand miles to see her though I feared flying; how I gave up a newspaper career for the idea of writing, though I loved newspapers.

I never felt alone in Manila. It was impossible to feel alone. There was instant connection with everything around me, and I was no longer watching from a safe distance, no longer an outsider. Sometimes I saw myself in Filipinos. There was a kinship, like family, people you have known a long time, forever. We had superficial things in common: the tropics, bloodlines to Spain, deep bonds to the Roman Catholic Church and with America. I had a natural understanding of their culture that did not come from books. There was the colonial's craving for acceptance and place, and I smiled knowingly at their fatalism. They called it *bahalina*—que será será—throwing themselves at the mercy of the gods, a sentiment so ingrown, so Asian and so Spanish both, that it came to them, it seemed, with birth itself. I understood too their flair for tragedy, their affinity for it, that life was opera, bombastic emotion, tear-drenched. And in the vigil that was their lives, I understood their search for deliverance—saints, astrology, tarot, dance.

But it was more than that, something far more alluring: a seduction. It was the hallucination of the tropics, the madness of the South Seas. The longing for the primitive and primal. A simple thing, perhaps, that allows a shedding of skin and a wild abandon. For me it came instantly, when I first saw Manila.

We had not been apart in six months, had not left the Philippines, but now Elizabeth was in Taiwan on a quick five-day trip she didn't want to make. The gray cast of temperate latitudes brought her nothing but gloom, nights of insomnia and days of dull interviews with thin-lipped men in black suits.

At a loss without her, I spent hours at the hotel. You could always tell when the foreign press thought nothing was going on in Manila. They had lunch by the pool. Over on one side were Kay and Camille, chatting at a table under the banyan tree where the pool attendants stood idle. On the other end, by the sunken pool bar, was Nick's table. Nick spotted me, came over for a cigarette, swinging on the balls of his feet.

"What have you done with Whitney?" he said, joking, looking around for her. It had been a long time since that night at La Taverna when Nick had blurted out to me that she was like tear gas, toxic. He had changed his mind working around her, getting to know her, maybe because he liked me, too. Now he was solicitous, caring, always looking after us.

"The desk wanted her to get out of the country and write about something else," I told him, and throwing his arm around me, he commiserated. He had to deal with the same demands from his bosses. Just then, when he was about to draw up a chair, he noticed a famous American writer, one of a handful who showed up from time to time to write about Cory Aquino. The writer, balding and paunchy with hairy legs, who had earned his reputation in Vietnam, was surrounded by an entourage of young, eager reporters lying on lounge chairs under a droopy magnolia tree, and Nick rushed off to join them.

Coming into the apartment from the pool later that day, I had to blink to keep from imagining Elizabeth standing there in her Manila Yacht Club T-shirt, ruffling my hair and making me listen to a Youssou N'Dour tape she had picked up at the mall. She was forever discovering music, obscure people who within months became stars.

I tried to go about my business while she was in Taiwan, and wrote for a number of hours each day, working on a piece about the political crisis in the country. The string of coup attempts, the bloody communist insurgency, the largest in Asia, a Muslim insurrection in the south. The country was splintering, no longer held together by the force of Marcos. Squatter camps sprouted all over Manila, rising up alongside five-star hotels and million-dollar condos. Beggars were getting younger and younger, and violence was a staple of daily life, something you shrugged off. Carjackings, kidnappings, and drug rings were run out of police stations, and in the provinces warlords and machete-happy cults terrorized peasants.

Cory Aquino was reeling: blows from the left, blows from the right. There was a slim middle as firm as quicksand where she stood. This was at a time—hard to imagine now, so many years later—when Cory was still a heroine to much of the world, adulated by the foreign press, *Time*'s "Woman of the Year."

I rewrote my piece countless times. Looked up a raft of notes I had taken at all those *merienda* interviews and on a trip with Elizabeth and Camille to a leftist mountain hamlet on the island of Panay. And I wove into the story the things I had heard in the Lobby Lounge and at the coffee shops around town, at the Inter-Continental and the Peninsula, where the coup backers, a handful of embittered politicians, financiers, and right-wing columnists, would take you aside and draw diagrams on paper napkins. After weeks of work, I mailed off the story to several magazines on the East Coast, feeling the combination of relief and anxiety that comes with a finished story.

It was then that I wrote a one-sentence note, addressed to no one but meant for Elizabeth. *Someday I will be able to write, because I will have to, about the years in which I knew you.*

She flew back from Taiwan the day before my birthday to surprise me. But she didn't find me at the apartment, there to rush to, to squeeze the back of my neck, and when I finally turned up, after an evening with Kay and Camille at the Weinstube, Elizabeth was sitting in the dark, waiting.

"I didn't know what it would be like," she said, bewildered, "coming home and you not here."

I walked over to her and raised her chin toward me and, bending down, kissed the soft flesh under her earlobe. A year had passed since my birthday on the bamboo raft at Matabungkay, and I was now having my second birthday in Manila. That evening Elizabeth took me to the Cowrie Grill at the Manila Hotel, the restaurant we liked for special occasions. We sat at our table toward the back, with floating candleholders and sprigs of baby orchids, and we had raw oysters and champagne and French Cabernet, red drops on her lips.

6

HOW QUICKLY WE disassemble our lives. The apartment at Del Pilar had been our cloister, but now we wanted a house, trees, a garden, a bigger sky at our windows.

We found an old wooden house in a compound a couple of miles up Roxas Boulevard, farther out from the city. It had a yard with frangipani trees and tamarinds, marigolds and bougainvillea. Elizabeth had longed for the outdoors: she missed her garden back home, the sense of space that came with a house and many rooms, porches to sit on, and birds to track.

We saw the house off Roxas one day when we went over to visit Camilla, who lived alone with her pug and her maid in the compound, diagonally across from a house that would soon be vacant, number 33. It was the first in a cluster of four houses on an unpaved two-car lane. The houses were wonderful relics from colonial times, unlike anything I had seen in downtown Manila, draped in bamboo stands, palm fronds, and yucca leaves. The compound had no name, but we called it P. Lovina, the name of the street that ran alongside it, a stretch of dilapidated motels, food stalls, and squatter huts, a block off the bay.

From outside, the house seemed oddly askew, with curved bays north and south. It stood a bit lopsided, as if one side had sunk inches deeper into the ground over decades of floods. Cypress green patches showed in spots through a thin coat of white paint that was already flaking, and the slanted tin roof was rusting. Set back from P. Lovina, with only a sagging wire fence to protect it from passersby, the house rose high off the ground, almost two stories, with the lower exterior enclosed by flimsy wood slats nailed in a crisscross pattern, giving them the appearance of a garden trellis. Bordering the foot of the house were overgrown rosebushes, bare patches strewn with broken glass, and a tangle of weeds. A shroud of old trees cast large shadows over a yard that had been left to the seasons. And around the front, where a garage door opened to an empty, unfinished ground floor, an awning of tin scraps hung over the maroon-colored steps that led up to a wide, screened veranda cooled by the breeze.

From the moment we swerved into the dirt driveway and ran up the steps of the house, Elizabeth wanted it. She waltzed from room to room, throwing doors open, sticking her head in the bathroom, measuring the rooms in her head: a sunny living room with beamed ceilings and wide-plank floors, bleached cedar walls and Capiz-shell window shutters; an airy kitchen; a sunlit room for my study; and our bedroom, with high windows open to the side yard. There was a raw beauty about the place, and a feeling that it would soon come to ruin. Winds had blown too hard against it, and time, too. But for us, it seemed ideal, secluded and unspoiled.

We would have dinners and parties, and we would smell blooms all around us and feel the rain directly overhead, sometimes hard like stones crashing on the tin roof, like the ripe coconuts that dropped off from time to time, rolling down and waking us, and we could see sky from every room.

We moved in May, a large van taking our things, dishes and pans, the office stuff that Gina and her sister Edna had spent days wrapping in newspapers and packing while Elizabeth and I rushed about our apartment, marking up boxes and checking off our lists, the tape deck blasting at full volume. The movers came and cushioned the furniture in quilts, strapped desk drawers, and hauled down the sofa and our bed, the steamer trunk, and all the rest. The building's maids and janitors stood around gaping. I had moved a dozen times and this was the fastest move I had seen, leaving us suddenly in a bare apartment, as if we had never lived there at all.

Over the ten months we had lived there together we had collected restored pieces Elizabeth bargained for in the antique shops along Mabini Street and in the galleries in Intramuros, the old Spanish fortress city within Manila. She had found a hand-carved Mindanao bird, a Chinese chest, altar tables, and a narrow onetime chicken coop, made of wood, that had been converted into a long bench, which now would occupy the length of a wall in our new bedroom at P. Lovina. We had our butaca and the Rajasthani chairs, and Elizabeth had pillows made for those chairs and had them upholstered in hand-spun indigo cottons she had bought in Sri Lanka. In time we brought an Afghan rug and an Iranian tapestry from Hong Kong, and a statuette of a Buddhist monk with a beggar's bowl and a gold-leaf goat sculpture from Bangkok, and a pair of long wall carvings that had been smuggled out of Burma into Thailand.

I was turning the small back room into my study, with a view of the bayside palm trees and the bay's spectacular sunsets and the rosebushes at my window. I had a twin bed, a glass-fronted bookcase, a big bulletin board, an electric typewriter. I had windows on two sides and the rustling of tree leaves in the breeze. Elizabeth made the screened veranda in front of the house into her office, just as she had once transformed her Manila Hotel room, thumbtacking flags, calendars, and maps, arranging a workplace in a corner open to the wind, the sun, the rain, and the constant noise of traffic going by on P. Lovina. She got a scratched-up desk the compound's owner gave her, and a bookcase she had dragged from New Delhi was her file cabinet. She had a straight-backed chair and her computer and her old Royal. She gave me—a birthday present—a hand-tooled *narra* (mahogany) swivel chair and her New Delhi desk, and these completed my study.

We had not wanted a staff, a household of full-time help, and we had not needed both Gina and Edna, but Gina said she would not move without her sister. We had room for them, in the maids' quarters below the kitchen stairs. We were tired of restaurants, and Elizabeth, who hated to waste money, wanted to eat at home more often, as she had done when she lived alone, making herself dinners of beans or soup. But the house was too big for the two of us to care for, and we hardly thought we wanted beans or soup for dinner every night. We were too busy to do the cleaning and grocery shopping ourselves, and Gina begged us to bring Edna along, so we hired Edna too.

She was older than Gina, plain-looking, flat-faced and stocky, a square body on short legs, and Gina had the oval face of a young virgin and a coquettish eye. Unlike Gina, Edna spoke no English and had no experience working for gringos. But she was a talent at the stove, turning out feasts for us and our guests. She could make lemon chicken and grilled lapu-lapu, frying the fish to a crisp the way I liked it, or broiling it in olive oil and garlic. These were not basic Filipino dishes. These were dishes Elizabeth taught her to make, communicating in a language of their own, mincing garlic, slicing mushrooms, tasting as they went along. Edna had a specialty all her own, the Filipino eggroll they call lumpia. It was a triumph, and Edna knew it. She would come out of the kitchen in her pressed apron with a cocky smile, her small hands balancing platters heaped with fried rolls, which were devoured by our guests, who left oil stains from the lumpia on the carpet and the white sofa.

Mornings she would knock softly on our door, carrying a tray of coffee and the newspapers. We never left our room until we were dressed, living as we were with eyes all around us. Elizabeth was no longer free to run around half naked, but she was still first in the bathroom, leaving me to my newspapers, and by the time I got in the shower there was no hot water left, or any water at all. I would scream out the window, *"Tubig! Tubig!"* ("Water! Water!"), and Edna would run next door and get the housekeeper there, Nanette, to turn off their hot-water pipes. The compound's water tower and plumbing worked just as unreliably as the city's, with its regular brownouts and rare garbage pickups.

I had grown up with servants, but that was a long time ago, and here in Manila I had found it uncomfortable having maids. I didn't like giving orders and found myself trying to befriend

Edna and Gina, treating them with respect and deference. Once I surprised Gina in the kitchen, started a conversation, but I had interrupted her reverie in the middle of the day and she looked up at me sullenly. She had defiance in her, a quiet rancor that made me watch out. Edna was the opposite, talkative (with her eyes and hands, and in Tagalog), spry at all hours, eager to mend a tear in my clothes, to run to the stall for my cigarettes, to deal with the plumber or the guy who trucked in our cases of beer. She kept the house humming. Because I liked her so, I tried not to notice the subtle changes I saw in her expression when Gina was around. She became stiff and dour with us. There were a few times when they were cleaning together and saw Elizabeth and me sitting side by side, our heads close, our hands almost touching, and I would catch Gina glancing over at Edna, a quick exchange that instinctively made me pull away from Elizabeth.

We had a theory of life below stairs, what we called the culture of the maids — *las criadas del siglo,* we called them, maids of the century. Nanette, Becky, Florence, our neighbors' live-in housekeepers, kept an eye on newcomers, on the traffic in and out of the compound. After their day's work they gathered, laughing and whispering, in the backyard or in Nanette's room next door. Nanette was the elder, the majordomo of the servants. They knew everything that went on in those houses: they overheard the lovers' quarrels through thin walls, they knew how many bottles of gin were consumed and who slept with whom. The maids, not us, I used to say, really ran the compound.

In the apartment on Del Pilar, Elizabeth and I had worked a few feet apart, interrupting each other, reading aloud, trying out

ideas. But now we had a living room between us, a formal ar-
rangement, as formal as we could become, careful not to distract
each other.

Working alone in my study, gazing out the windows—cloudy
skies, bright skies, street traffic—or lying on the twin bed I had
there for overnight guests, watching the ceiling fan blades ro-
tate, waiting in vain for the flow of words to start, was more
distracting than having Elizabeth nearby. I could easily fritter
away time. I fixed up the room, rearranged my books, put things
up on a wall board: the Cory doll, banners, postcards, poolside
pictures.

On the days when she was home writing, I overheard cackles,
a screech, the phone slamming, some excitement of hers, and
three, four times, she came into my room. She made it a point
to be brisk: laid her hands on my shoulders, flipped through my
pages, gave me a story of hers to look over, related some news
she had heard. With some excuse—that I needed to stretch my
legs—I would leave my room and go see her, poking my head
out to the porch and pulling up a chair next to hers. One day
I caught her drawing, something she started doing in Manila,
pen and crayon doodles in her appointment book, tennis courts,
airplanes, birds, herself with hair like flames. Her moods, black
clouds, brilliant suns.

Around midday, when the sharp smell of Edna and Gina's rice
and pastis lunch seeped through the house, Edna would bring us
a plate of chopped-egg sandwiches and a couple of San Miguels.
Without saying a word, she placed everything on Elizabeth's
desk, backed away, and waited at the doorway to the living
room, her hands folded in front of her, for instructions on the

grocery list, the menu for the evening, a bottle of gin, cigarettes. Then she padded down the front steps, smoothing down her hair and the wrinkles in her uniform, humming, off to the market.

All day long there were doors banging, cars pulling in and out of the dirt drive in front of Elizabeth's office. Dogs barked, a pair of snarling whippets that guarded the compound but mainly preyed on the cats. Maids shuffled in and out, washing clothes in their tubs, whistling, singing. From my back office I could hear Gina waxing our floors with her coconut husk, and early in the morning we were awakened by the whoosh of Edna's broom and the cluck of the rooster that the compound's armed sentry kept in our front yard. Only the gardener made no noise. He walked on bare feet, spoke only when he came up to be paid, sticking out a reedy arm and mumbling apologetically about a sick son, but the rest of the day he kept his head down, hunched over the rosebushes, clipping the grass blade by blade with his scissors.

Chaotic Manila had been relatively quiet all that summer, our first three months at P. Lovina. There were no rumors of coups after the one in late 1986 that fizzled even before it got started. There was no news of massacres or ferries sinking or guerrilla attacks in the provinces, where an old Muslim insurrection festered in the far south of Mindanao and the largest communist insurgency in Asia survived in the central islands. With my writing coming more easily, though I had yet to sell a piece, my bleak moods and the fights that followed had grown smaller, fleeting like the migraines I had had for many years. With the rainy season in the offing, the summer seemed to fly by with friends and the daily routine of writing and filing.

Elizabeth, having grown up with cocktail parties and formal dinners, cared little for the social whirl. She had enough of it going out every day on her news rounds. But for me, closeted in the house most of the day, going out was a relief. I needed the political talk, the ferocious arguments, the late nights, all that smoke and wine that we enjoyed at Sandro's, next door.

Sandro was a sixties radical, had come to Manila from Italy to work on an engineering project in the Marcos years. He stayed one year, then two, more than a decade, found love with a Filipina model, divorced, and was now living with Candy, a tall, striking Filipina American who had grown up with cover-girl looks and money. Sandro had long ago given up engineering and had become a news photographer, working for European and American magazines, taking pictures all over Southeast Asia. He made plenty of money, lived like a pasha, knew everyone in town, and even in his fifties had the virile good looks of Italian matinée idols. He still showed off a flat stomach and muscled frame. Even if his hair was graying and thinning, he was one of the best-looking foreigners in Manila—Sandro and New Delhi Nick had the swagger.

Those evenings at Sandro's were long and heavy, an excess of rich food, drink, and talk. He usually wore his evening outfit, a colorful sarong he had picked up in Burma and a hip-long white linen tunic, and hosted these gatherings on his candlelit porch, which he had enclosed and decorated with Asian masks and artifacts, creating the illusion of an opium den. Puffing on a smoke, he conducted the conversation like a symphony maestro, while Candy, who rarely said much around him, played with her hair and sipped wine. Elizabeth and I always stayed longer than we planned and got home across the yard past midnight and a bit wobbly, the smell of incense in our hair and clothes.

On weekends when the weather was good, Sandro would drive out in his tennis whites, screeching to a stop at our doorstep, letting us into the car for the ride to the Manila Hotel. Courtside, Candy and I drank mango juice and sunned our legs and gossiped about whatever was the latest scandal. Sandro was a screamer on the court, shouting when he made every shot, his face streaked in sweat, headband and polo shirt soaked, and Elizabeth — who matched him grunt for grunt, a racket-thrower herself, merciless in combat — scrambled, leaped, raced, a storm on the court. She was younger and fast but not as strong, and just when she was about to beat him, his knees crunching, he got it out of his gut and something in her pulled back and he would win. "Elisabetta! *Bella!*" he called out to her in his Italian accent, spreading his sweaty arms around her slim shoulders, his six feet bent protectively over her.

We had long dinners at La Taverna, bottles of Chianti drunk with pasta putanesca and all'Amatriciana, simple, old-fashioned Italian dishes that seemed glorious after days of mahi-mahi, sticky fried rice, kare-kare, and pork adobo. Sandro, who had spent fifteen years in the Philippines, entertained us with a stream of stories. He had married and divorced after some scandal he was mysterious about. In Candy he'd found another perfectly sexy companion. She had the tossed long hair, shapely legs, the bikini figure of a model, and had a weekly manicure and pedicure, regular facials and waxing, and beauty naps, and wore satin camisoles. They made a striking couple, elegant and tall in sunglasses.

Presiding at his dinners at home like a sultan in his sarong, tinkling the bell for Nanette and the cook to serve, Sandro made us his sounding board, wrapped up like him in the dirty politics and brutality of the place. "When I came here, this was the third world. Now it's worse than Bangladesh." He laughed. "Now it's the fifth world."

He was at the point, a threshold often reached by foreigners in the tropics, at which contempt replaces infatuation with the exotic. Locals, once seeming so hospitable and engaging, become, over time, transfigured into ignorant inferiors, mulish, too brown, too dirty, too greedy, shifty-eyed. Corruption, which at first is intriguing and acceptable after four centuries of colonialism and miserable poverty, becomes a character flaw, ingrained in the locals like a genetic blood disease. Their dreaminess, the way they turn a funeral into a fiesta, which had once charmed, now seems pagan and uncivilized. Their colors become too loud, their manners crude, their language primitive. Sandro had reached that point. "This is not a country," he would say, lobbing an insult while speeding down Roxas Boulevard, shouting at the beggars. "This is a collection of tribes."

Candy sat by cringing, raising her voice to defend her country, knowing she could not, and he would shut her up. Oddly, she was the foreigner among us, the Westerners who were guests in her country. But when Sandro was away on a photo shoot, Candy would come over to our house with a bottle of wine and fill our ashtrays with red-lipsticked butts, telling us *cuentos,* stories that kept us glued to her for hours. Like many a good-looking woman, she had her struggles with men, her wild days as a Makati beauty, and now her boring days at the travel office where she worked. She wanted to marry Sandro, have children, a home, but there was no way Sandro would agree. He was more worried about his thinning hair, his aching legs, and losing his edge in the field. He didn't know how much more bloodshed he could stomach, but he loved Manila in his way, with that bitter love that he knew would hang on to him forever. I could see it written on his face when Candy talked about traveling with him to Italy to visit, to meet his family. He would abruptly leave the room, turn up the volume on the music on his tape player, and change the subject of conversation altogether.

In late afternoons, when nothing else was happening, we crossed over to Camilla's house down the lane. There were slices of mango, chocolates, crackers, gin and tonics, and she would show Elizabeth the brilliant fabrics she had discovered in her trips to Mindanao and Bangkok. Camilla wrapped them around her hipless waist, trying them out for color and shade. An intuitive photographer, Camilla had no fixed ambition, no direct route anywhere. She usually had a project going—reupholstering her sofa, stripping old wooden frames, saving strays in the yard—when she wasn't traveling out in the islands, sometimes with Elizabeth, taking pictures of military camps and homeless villagers, massacres and shootouts, for a photo agency in London. But there were times we found her in her bedroom, blinds drawn, reading a romance novel, and times when she could not stop pacing from room to room, screaming at her maid for failing to buy groceries, or yelling into a dead telephone after a call home.

She had gone to a boarding school, dropped out, spent summers in the Bahamas or Bermuda and winters in Aspen or the Alps, stayed at the Pierre in New York, but seemed just as comfortable in a provincial motel in Panay or a toiletless shack in the mountains. She traveled first class with her Louis Vuitton luggage or on a jeepney with a knapsack. I often thought there was about her an only child's loneliness.

Afternoons when I couldn't write and Elizabeth was out, I would visit Camilla and bore her with the latest report on my work. It was important to me that friends knew I was hard at work, that I was writing, that I was *doing* something. She paid attention, trying to figure out what it was that I was writing. Then we drifted to other things and I would lose her interest. I didn't enjoy the trust she had in Elizabeth, to whom she confided. So we were left with bolts of fabric to discuss, but I was useless in this area—fabrics and recovering cushions and sofas and those things that interested her and Elizabeth, at least on the surface. It's beautiful, I always remarked when she unfolded the cloth, asking if the colors would go with the new slipcovers, the kind of question that I had picked up from listening to her and Elizabeth for hours.

Around dusk, when the breeze increased and the leaves of the bamboo stalks that grew around Camilla's veranda brushed against her porch screen, I would run down her steps and up the pebbled lane just as Elizabeth was arriving home. She would immediately throw off her bag and loosen her shoes and Edna would bring us chilled glasses of San Miguel and we would stretch out on the rattan sofa, catching up on our day. Far, far from us, I could still hear the wail of the birds' eggs vendor on P. Lovina, crying *"Balut, balut."*

Rejection letters came from all the magazines to which I had sent my political piece. One by one, each rejection slip went up on my bulletin board. I tried to find encouragement where there was none. One magazine editor sent me back the manuscript with a terse note saying she already had a writer, a name I recognized, reporting from Asia, and that my article was, with regret, being sent back unread.

Elizabeth had saved her rejection letters for years, as many writers do, believing rejection was part of what they call the journey. But she glanced over that especially insulting letter, frowning, saying it was unbelievable that the editor hadn't even bothered to skim my piece. I sulked, glaring at her as if this were her fault, and went off to the fridge for a beer.

"It's going to take you six years," she said calmly, pouring beer into our glasses. Was this one of her visions? Why six, why not five or ten? It was 1987. Did I have to wait until 1993? "I just know," she said flatly. "I can't see these things about myself, but I always know about you." I didn't know if I believed her, but I knew she believed it. Crooking her forefinger into mine, sitting close to me, she said, "You are a writer—of that, maybe only about that, I am certain."

But I felt that time was running out for me, and my money was almost gone. I had been supporting myself with the money from the sale of my house, but that money was going fast. Around this time, Kay was called back by the network she had been working for and would be leaving Manila soon. She took me to L'Orangerie, a fancy restaurant where society matrons stopped for lunch with their Rustan's shopping bags. Over her cup of *halo-halo*, she gossiped briefly about some scandal at ABC. Then, dipping her dessert spoon into the glop of jackfruit, flan, and purple yam ice cream, she dropped a bomb on me. You should go back to the States, she said, get a job. Ignoring the look of shock on my face, she went on. "You can't stay here doing nothing. It will kill you." I wanted to lean over the table and knock her head off, but instead I nodded unhappily.

Later I had to admit that I was floundering, snapping at Elizabeth, turning my frustration against her. Just when things were looking grim, my stack of typed pages looking ridiculous, like such a vain dream, work came along. A reporter for the *San Francisco Chronicle* was leaving Manila and she recommended me for her job.

Within days, I was off to South Korea. For years, student demonstrations had been a fixture of the Seoul spring season, marking the massacre in Kwangju in the 1960s, but this time the anti-government movement was much larger, involving tens of thousands of militants, students and middle-class professionals, men and women, young and old. The uprising in a country known for rigid and bloody governments was getting front-page headlines in Asia and in the West. The military-backed government, which had ruled the country for more than twenty years, was on the verge of falling, teetering dangerously. Every foreign correspondent in Manila was rushing to Seoul (as were correspondents from Tokyo, Bangkok, Beijing). Elizabeth had a visa and a plane ticket ready to go, and leaped out of her chair when I told her I was going with her. The *Chronicle* was sending me, all expenses paid. I had business cards printed and got a visa and a plane ticket and packed my khaki jacket and notebooks, stuffing a duffel bag. We had no idea how long we would be gone, figured on a week or ten days. Excited as I was, and scared to cover such a big story, I knew that the life of a correspondent was not exactly what I had had in mind when I thought of writing books, but it was quite a score, and I was thrilled.

It was June 1987, and the scrubbed streets of Seoul, swept down to the last scrap, had been turned into a battleground by tens of thousands of youths in scarves, carrying shards of pavement and broken bricks in their hands. From our room at the Seoul Hilton, we looked down on the wide boulevards that at the moment seemed orderly, with white traffic stripes designating areas for pedestrian traffic at corners and intersections. Seoul was all black and white, like a charcoal drawing. White for the students, the white of their T-shirts, the white of the surgical masks they wore to keep from breathing in tear gas; and black for the government troops: black helmets, black shields, black uniforms.

We had left our hilltop hotel and were running down the slope toward the downtown streets, weaving in and out of the student columns, when tear gas canisters started popping from tanks shooting projectiles toward the students. Rocks and hunks of brick and sidewalk concrete flew in the air and crash-landed everywhere, clanking against police shields, on helmets, on students and reporters. Over here was a student moaning in pain, with a bloody face, his head smashed, being carried out of the line of fire by other students. Over there was the unbroken line

of helmeted troops raising their thick shields to protect themselves against the rain of bricks and stones. We ran, crouching,
our arms over our heads, faces down, and found a safe spot behind a building. I thought my head was going to burst. People
were screaming, running in all directions. *Pop-pop!* The canisters kept coming, splattering on the pavement and blasting the
skin. Government troops didn't use real bullets, but the tear gas
was tough, war grade, like mustard gas. I felt it could tear out my
lungs.

The next day we went prepared for anything, wearing mil-
itary-like helmets and U.S. Army gas masks that we'd bought
in a shop downtown where reporters geared up. Sweat and
breath fogged up my goggles, and I had to take big gulps of air
when the tear gas canisters exploded, spreading puffs of stinging
smoke. The tear gas was dense, nauseating, and I was coughing,
couldn't hear myself speak. I lost track of Elizabeth and wandered around side streets looking for her. My heart was pumping
madly, but I got far enough from the clouds of gas to take my
mask off. I was queasy, sick to my stomach. Slowly, trying to
orient myself on unfamiliar streets, without a map, I found the
way to Myeongdong Cathedral, a center of anti-government ac-
tivity. I found Elizabeth there, seated on the steep steps up a hill,
her hair plastered down, her mask stuffed in her bag, interview-
ing students.

That afternoon I filed my first story to San Francisco, a
straight news account that I wrote in a nervous frenzy, chain-
smoking and pounding on the desk when the words didn't come.
When the editors in San Francisco told me it was leading the

front page, I let out a howl and Elizabeth raised a wineglass in my direction and, beaming, said, "You know, you might be better at this than I am."

We were still in Seoul three weeks later when the final round of the uprising came at the end of June. President Chun Doo Hwan, humiliated by the swelling opposition, which now included world leaders as well as the South Korean corporate and middle class, stepped down. A former general, ghostly in a dark suit, he went on state television and gave a speech that was stirring not for its tenor, as he was emotionless, but because of the words he wielded—*free elections, civilian rule*. It sent shock waves across the peninsula and reached all around the world.

That evening we took off with the boys to the Bear House, a distinctive tavern set in the thick green hills outside the city. At my left sat the *New York Times* and at my right the *San Jose Mercury News*, and we had wine and big slabs of beef and I listened to the stories around the table, telling some of my own, shoptalk, chuckling, everyone puffed up. It was a long, roaring, blowsy evening. Across the table, Elizabeth gazed at me with a smile, making it my night.

Time moved so fast then, and the choices I had to make that summer caught me off-guard. It had been a year since I had moved to Manila, and here was another August so soon. On our return from Seoul I had a letter reminding me that my leave of absence was expiring.

I ripped open the envelope knowing full well the news it was bringing me, read the short formal letter quickly, and, clutching it, stood in front of Elizabeth, who had been seated at her desk, working. I handed her the letter. She scanned it, looked up at me, and said, "So soon." She had a year and a half left in her tour—a year and a half in which we would live apart. Eighteen months of letters and telephone calls and that awful empty longing. "Impossible!" I said out loud. I remembered too clearly the last time we had been apart, the summer of 1986, when I slept on my sofa, the telephone perched on an armrest nearby so I could fling my hand on the phone the second it rang. I remembered too well the fluorescent lights in the office, the lonely pasta dinners, and the Manila Blues tapes.

I was propped up on cushions in the bedroom that evening when Elizabeth came out of the shower, her long hair pulled up, a towel rolled around her waist and chest. Drops of water trickled down between her shoulder blades and down the curve of her back. I watched her pour lotion on the palms of her hands, rub them together and up her forearms and shoulders, up to the swerve of her neck, then down her legs. She didn't seem aware of my eyes as she fluttered among her things, doing her ritual ablutions. She slid in on her side of the bed, pushing the lightweight cotton Indian blanket down to her feet.

"Are you crying?" Her voice was low, a whisper. She moved closer, touched a teardrop on my cheek, and took my face in her hands. She could let me go, she said. She could handle it, she said.

I tried to find a way to stay, and I called up the managing editor to tell him I would go back but only to work as a reporter, not as an editor. Why don't you fly back and we'll talk about it, he said to placate me. I knew that false ring in his voice. I knew the answer was no. They wanted me back on the Foreign Desk.

I waited silently, thought of a future without a newspaper job and no money. He had won. I would fly back to talk it over. I made plans to go; Elizabeth decided to go with me. Nothing was happening in Manila, and she wanted time off. I called Tim to tell him. It had been a long time since we had talked, and hearing his booming voice and his effusive enthusiasm reminded me of our old talks in the row house. He wanted me to stay at his place, and Andy, who was also living there, would pick me up at the airport. We were packing our bags late the night before takeoff on August twenty-seventh when the phone rang.

Malacañang was under attack, someone yelled into the phone. We got Camilla out of bed. We woke up Candy next door. The first thing Candy said was, "Sandro's in Italy! He will hate himself for missing this." Camilla grabbed her cameras and the four of us piled into Candy's car and sped down Roxas Boulevard toward the presidential palace about two miles away. The roads were empty. Red flares flashed across the sky. In the distance there was gunfire. Heavily armed soldiers in black berets—the elite presidential guard—surrounded Malacañang and the entrance nearby to Arlegui Street, where Cory Aquino lived. A handful of local reporters and gawkers milled about. Taking out my notebook, I asked the people around me if they knew if the president was safe. They shrugged, shaking their heads. Elizabeth moved into the street crowd, questioning bystanders and the few guards who allowed her to approach. No one knew anything. The soldiers pushed us back, shouting, "Clear out! Clear out!"

It was already past two in the morning, pitch black, strangely quiet suddenly. We drove off to Camp Aguinaldo, some three miles from the palace. The streets around the camp were deserted. A six-wheeled truck was parked crossways near the main gate, blocking the way. We got out of the car and walked cautiously toward the truck and ran smack into a couple hundred men in black ski masks and bandoliers, carrying M16s and M60s. They were massed at a side gate to the camp, pushing their way in. For months we had been waiting for the big coup, the one that was going to end Cory's presidency, and we also knew it had been drawn up, plotted and directed by a flashy colonel we had interviewed six months earlier. These were his men. This was his coup. That much we knew.

By dawn, a clear, steamy day, crowds had gathered around the camp and on the eight-lane EDSA, the Epifanio de los Santos Avenue that had played such a big role as the site of mass demonstrations during the People Power Revolution. Gawkers, *mirones,* and kids climbed up over the high barbed-wire fence, running not away from but toward the sounds of shooting. Television crews, local reporters, foreign correspondents, and photographers were spread out through the crowd, crouching up and down EDSA along the front entrance to the camp. I was standing with a large crowd when I heard and then felt a bullet whip past my ear. First I felt the wind, the whoosh. Then I heard the crack. I saw a column of soldiers moving toward us, and I grabbed Elizabeth and charged down a street, my heart racing. The pavement shook under the slaps of hundreds of running shoes and rubber sandals. Elizabeth sprinted ahead of me, pulling me forward, and the shooting did not stop. We ran down a side street of shabby homes and there we found a car to take us back home to P. Lovina. Drained, exhausted, and soaked with sweat, I filed a story to the San Francisco paper while Elizabeth worked at her desk on the screened-in porch.

No one would agree later at what point the coup failed, whether reinforcements from the north did not come through or the coup leaders flinched at the last moment, arriving at Cory Aquino's home without the nerve to capture her. But when it was over, the headquarters of the armed forces of the Philippines lay in ruins: shelled, pounded, and finally incinerated. Rebel soldiers came out waving white flags, stumbling and falling, hiding their faces, a defeated army. It was the bloodiest fighting in Manila—some sixty people killed—since World War II.

We canceled our trip to the States, and, making the decision I had known all along I would have to make, I let my leave of absence expire. My days as a foreign editor were over.

For the crowd of foreign reporters and photographers who had lived through the last months of Marcos and the madness of the revolution in 1986, the coup attempt of August 1987 was the last great explosion, the moment, so undefinable, when the story turned. In the next few months there was hardly a peaceful week, a dull day. The coup attempt had attracted notoriety worldwide, and I was filing stories to San Francisco almost every day and getting raves from the *Chronicle* editors.

A chaotic metropolis in the best of times, Manila seemed overcome with anger and sinister conspiracy theories. A friend of ours, a young leftist leader named Lean, was assassinated in broad daylight, his face blown away by bullets from a passing van while he was on his way to make a speech. Cory Aquino, who barely escaped from the coup attempt with her life, once again shook up her administration. Cabinet secretaries were fired, generals shuffled, captains and lieutenants we knew were placed under armed guard in their own homes. Aquino, looking ashen and haggard after such a close call, took on a steely military pose, no longer wearing her canary yellow smocks and prattling away about peace and reconciliation.

Saturated with Manila and feeling after-coup fatigue, we made plans to take December off and go to the States. Edna and Gina, who would stay to take care of our house, squealed with joy when we gave them their Christmas presents—clothes and money. Their eyes teary, they watched us get into a car waiting to take us to the airport. Standing straight and proud in their pink uniforms, with their faces pressed to the porch screen, Edna cradled Boom, a scrawny orange stray kitty Camilla had given Elizabeth for Christmas, her parting gift before she left for London for the holidays. Looking up at Boom and the girls, I swung open the taxi door and slid into the back seat, doing the mental travel checklist—passport, wallet, plane ticket, dollars—distracting myself. The car turned the corner and I looked back at the girls, the squatters in the vacant lot next to our house, the domino players in the shed, the waters of the bay.

7

MORNINGS OVER FRESH coffee, and late-night catch-up sessions with Andy, my voice a rasp, filled my first days back at Tim's house, which smelled of pine and Christmas candles left to melt in the night, wax spots on a coffee table. Already the tree was trimmed with cranberries and tinkling ornaments I'd found in one of the boxes I had stored in Tim's basement.

It had been two years since the day I left the suburbs and found a refuge in Orchard, and now my old friend and ally Andy occupied it, had watered the plants, hung new pans in the kitchen, put out fresh towels and soap for me. The city was enduring an arctic spell, and we had gone out, he and I, the day after my arrival, to find a tree, with muffs on my ears, scarf up to my nose. We bought gifts to put under it, and afterward, lights twinkling and pine drops in our hair, we sprawled happily on the sofa and sipped cups of hot rum.

Elizabeth and I had flown back together, but she had gone on to visit her parents in Connecticut, while I was going to Tim's and later on to Texas to spend a few Christmas days with my family.

Tim was returning from assignment in Afghanistan, where he had mounted mules, squatted down with mujahideen, scoured the bazaars of Kabul, and waited for coded signals in the mazes of Peshawar. He came back with a bushy beard and mustache, and a thicker waist. He had grown older, lines under his eyes, a slight sag to his cheeks, but his eyes had the moony spark of the road, of having been somewhere, and he hugged me, swallowed me in his arms, and he put on his muj turban for me and offered me the attic, his room, and he picked up the dirty socks under his bed and wiped the dust off the stacks of books on shelves and desks.

He stayed with us only a few days, shuttling here and there, sleeping on the sofa, hanging up the handmade carpets he brought from Islamabad, but mostly talking, a running mono-logue. He always talked out his stories, could recite full inter-views, and paint the backdrops.

Elizabeth called up every now and then from her parents' home, but only with the sparest conversations ending in breezy goodbyes. I rarely called her there, wounded every time her tone was that of someone talking to a stranger or a secretary, crisp and businesslike. For three weeks we had little contact, but I knew she was joining me before New Year's, and that made the days tolerable. We had agreed that she would visit her parents alone. She hadn't seen them in two years, their longest separation ever, and they had to talk privately and sort out all of their differences and disagreements, all of those things she knew would devastate them. She had to deal with this alone with them.

I saw old friends, tried out the latest restaurants, went to brunches, and flew to Texas for thirty-six hours to spend Christmas with my mother and sisters. I hadn't seen my family in three years, and in the interim everyone's lives had gone on in different directions. I was fortunate. I didn't have to explain anything to my family. They rarely questioned my decisions or my life even if at times I might have upset them. When I got back from Texas, I met with editors in New York and in Washington, discussing prospects, possibilities. Nothing was offered, and I could not see beyond that point ahead to a whole year—to the end of 1988—when Elizabeth's assignment in Manila would be over and we would have to return to America.

A couple of days before New Year's, I was alone in the house, my ears perking up at the sound of each car passing. Then I heard a car slow down and stop, turn in and out of a parking space. A car door slammed shut and steps came closer and stopped at our doorstep. The bell rang. I opened the door, and Elizabeth's face was brushing mine, her arms enclosing me.

Tim's attic had no lamps. The bed was covered in a heavy spread that smelled of age, sweat, and cologne, but the linen was fresh, and the room had the sheltering quiet of a garret. A streetlamp cast shifting shadows on the walls inside the attic, and above the rooftops across the way the pink light of the moon on a cloudy night fell faintly on the bed's pillows. I could make out the sharp edges of Elizabeth's cheeks, the corner of a closing eyelid, and a half shadow on the parting of her mouth.

I awoke the next morning to her eyes looking at me. She was propped up on her elbow, looking down on me, sunbeams angling across the bed. I pushed back the hair from her forehead.

I wrapped the quilt tighter around us. We had not had moments like this in our last frantic months in Manila, moments when, with nothing around us, we could languish undisturbed, submerged, alone.

On the night of New Year's Day, we had lobster and champagne. Elizabeth's eyeglasses steamed up as she bent over the deep pot, and after jumping back as she threw the live lobsters into boiling water, she watched the brown shells quickly turn brilliant pink. She melted the butter and, all done, poured herself a finger of Scotch. I had candles on the table and champagne glasses I'd found in my stored boxes, and I got fresh flowers. The house smelled of fudge she had baked, and calla lilies and beeswax. The Christmas tree lights making white dots on the walls.

At the table she played with the lobster, cracking the claws, forking out the meat, sucking the juice, and then, taking the joints left on my plate, she dug in until there was nothing left but scraps of broken shells. I had never seen anyone eat lobster with such intensity, and I laughed at her; we laughed over nothing the way we did when no one was around.

There were obligations. She had to talk to the top editors, make the rounds at the paper, and accept dinner invitations. Innocuous occasions, usually, but for her uncomfortable. Awkward being the center of attention, she would say. As she walked through the newsroom, reporters and editors, doing a double take, recognizing her, came up to her, complimenting her stories, wanting her to talk about her exotic adventures, the sort of thing she made a point of not doing. But it was not all raves and slaps on the back and kisses. Some of them, even old friends, did not quite know what to say to us. What could they say? Gossip about us had gone around. We did not fit the picture anymore. They knew her before she left for India, when she was married and I was only her editor. Now there was no husband, and I had flown off to Manila and we were living together. Everyone tiptoed around that, but they seemed more open to her, warmer and kinder, while for me there was barely contained reproach. I had crossed the line—I had fallen in love with a reporter, a married woman.

I was having lunch with a columnist who had been a casual friend before my move to Manila. It was just the two of us, and I had looked forward to seeing her and catching up. The lunch was going as most of those reunions go, a little awkward, a little forced and superficial but amenable overall. She was asking about Manila and Elizabeth when she lowered her voice and leaned toward me. "Are you a couple?" she said. "Everyone's talking about you two, so is it true, you're lovers?" I couldn't believe it and fell mute. What would Elizabeth say? I couldn't find the words, couldn't say yes. Finally I heard myself say, No, it isn't true. I didn't know who I was protecting. Me? Elizabeth? But it was too late to backtrack and explain. I had lied and I was ashamed of myself.

Elizabeth blew up at me. "How could you lie? Why, for god's sake?" I had been afraid, plain and simple, and lost my nerve. "You don't have people asking you that question," I lashed back. "You don't have to answer that question." The worst moment came when the managing editor, seated across from me at a long table in a windowless conference room, suggested without exactly saying so bluntly that I could not be rehired. My relationship with Elizabeth, he said, violated the paper's nepotism rule. He was red-faced, obviously embarrassed bringing up this subject. I was mortified, had no reply. I understood too well. They would keep her but cut me loose. I was the responsible guilty party. Later, when I told her, Elizabeth was shocked. How could they do that to you and not me? She threatened to quit the paper. I stopped her. I blamed myself. I had made the choice. When I had resigned at the end of my leave of absence, they had held out a hope that I could go back to the paper at some point. I had counted on that. I was wrong. People have to live with their choices, I liked to say. Now I had to live with mine. I had to start over.

It was January 1988 and our holiday was ending. Elizabeth did not take departures casually, and leaving her family again, the roads she loved driving on, the changes of season, her house outside the city, her ingrained American life, tore at her. We had a one-night stopover in Los Angeles before flying off to Manila, and we decided to step out of our hotel—the Biltmore—and its flashy cocktail bar and ambled without direction around the nearly empty downtown streets. We stopped at a Mexican restaurant that seemed to have some life in it and tried to make the evening stretch out, just a few more hours on American soil. At the same time, we were already nostalgic for Manila, knowing that the time was coming soon when our life there would end.

That was the year that Manila fell off the map. The story was fading. My editors in San Francisco had little appetite for Philippine stories, and many of the foreign correspondents were leaving Manila for bigger news in Hong Kong, Bangkok, Tokyo, the

Middle East. Nick was being transferred to New Delhi, the city of his old nightmares, where his wife had walked out on him after spending weeks alone in the heat while he traveled the subcontinent doing stories. He had been out in the field for nearly ten years, but he liked to say that he had two wars left in him and could not give up the life on the road, the sauced nights and midnight deadlines, dozing on airplanes from Madras to Nicosia. The *New York Times* and the *Washington Post* were planning to close their Manila offices, and a new breed of foreign correspondent was taking over the bureaus that remained in town. They were the early wave of the digital generation, earnest overachievers, straitlaced nonsmokers with black-frame glasses and dispassionate temperaments. Not a Nick in the bunch!

It seems to me that our life was a series of arrivals and departures, that we came together only to part; airports from San Francisco and Los Angeles to Bangkok to Seoul to Honolulu were familiar grounds. We had been back from the States less than two months, just enough time to feel at home again in our house on P. Lovina, when we were flying out of Manila again. This time Elizabeth was going to Sri Lanka for an indefinite period to work on a magazine story and I was going back to New York to get another job. I packed most of my things, believing that this could be it for my time in Manila. We thought about it that way, a separation we could no longer avoid or postpone. I would take a job and wait for her. We painted a silver lining on it to keep ourselves from unraveling, but those days were a touch melancholic, a series of unspoken goodbyes.

Sandro and Candy threw a blowout going-away party for me, and just about everyone came. To my surprise, I felt exuberant, embellishing the glories of New York. Slick in a black shirt and pants, her face blushed pink, Elizabeth held court in a corner, sunk into a floor cushion, mouthing cocktail patter with Nick, who had a new girlfriend, a soulful Californian who took pictures of the misery in Manila. Elizabeth behaved cheerfully enough, as if she had not a care in the world, but I could see her eyes wandering toward nothing in particular.

Our separation did not happen overnight. We made it a procession of days, days in Thailand, flying in a single-engine plane from Bangkok to Phuket, an island all green and lilac and magenta with bursts of flowers on the landing strip and along the route to our hotel, a hillside teak and stucco villa overlooking terraced gardens, the coral green and turquoise waters of the tan sand beach, and, farther in the distance, the royal blue of the Andaman Sea.

We spent three days sticking toes in the sand, sitting under canvas umbrellas, drinking tangy piña coladas. Her skin smelled of sea air and brine, and the late-afternoon sun filtered down on our room, slits of light through closed shutters, and in the open balcony, the ripple of vines.

Days later we sat restless and anxious in the waiting room at the airport in Bangkok, having nothing left to say after the last evening, after the dinner under torchlights at the riverside terrace of the Oriental Hotel, where we watched the barges churning slowly on the Chao Phraya, and later, in our room, curled under rose-perfumed sheets. I woke up a few hours later, shaking on the morning of my flight out.

It was time. We moved down the long corridors of the airport terminal to the departure gate as if we could slow down the clock. But I felt myself going numb, deliberately cutting her off, the need I had for her and the separation anxiety that seized me every time I boarded a plane. When the last call was announced, she slid the straps of the heavy bag she had carried for me on my shoulder. After the quickest of goodbyes, without an ardent embrace or even a casual hug, I stepped up to the security gate and laid my luggage on the conveyor belt and went through the metal checkpoint. I kept walking, looking straight ahead. I knew she was still standing behind the plate glass. I could feel her eyes on my back.

Flying out on Air France, I wrapped myself in smelly airline blankets and tried to sleep. I couldn't. I imagined her alone back at the hotel room at the Oriental, seated at the desk there, writing me already on the hotel's linen-soft stationery. She had noticed the minute she walked into the room that only one side of the bed had been turned down, that even the chambermaids knew I was no longer there. She ordered room service and drank to me, a glass of red wine. The next day she flew six hours to Colombo, Sri Lanka.

By now I was at Orchard House. The street and the buildings on it, even a dilapidated old church, looked just as shabby as they had looked when I lived there with Tim in the winter of 1986. It was two years later, but little had changed. Her letters from Sri Lanka arrived two, three times a week. Thin envelopes were addressed in her hand, with bird stamps — Ceylon's white-eye, Legge's flower pecker, Layard's parakeet.

She didn't believe I would stay gone and pictured instead having me there in Sri Lanka with her, getting a tan, flailing away at a tennis ball, and writing a book in my head. Pictures came, and brown envelopes bulging with patches of fabrics she liked, and her drawings, clippings from the Colombo newspapers, horoscopes, oddities. She wrote about her backbreaking car trip across the island's rough roads to the farthest northeastern point, the military encampments she visited, and the nights without sleep. There was the bar in Trincomalee, at the Seven-Islands Hotel, where everyone was drunk and jumpy, war at their door. Those hotels she stayed in were so easy for me to imagine — scratchy toilet paper, mosquito nets full of holes, swarms of bedbugs crawling over her legs, and her face sun-darkened, increasingly thin. She fell into the rhythm of the place, into a pace all her own.

This time Orchard could not save me. It felt hollow, a nest undone. I had little to do but spent a week trying out at the *Times*. On the first day, I wore a cashmere cardigan I had bought in Hong Kong and my only skirt and sat stiff as a board on a foldout chair in a windowless office. I held on my lap a folder with copies of articles I had written for the San Francisco paper, but no one asked to look at the clippings. They had no interest in my reporting. It was editing they had in mind for me. I had little choice but to go along. I went through the motions, making marks on copy rather casually, and left it at that. After five days, there were handshakes and thanks for my coming but there was no job offer. They said I would get their answer later, and, humbled, I walked out into Times Square.

The days and nights seemed interminable, and the friends I saw, the streets, everything about the city, had become distant.

Andy had a girlfriend; a wedding was planned and he was buying a house. Tim was away most of the time and had taken on
what seemed to me a somber manner, the Washington wonk in
him. He was distracted, pulled in every direction. He was starting a book and a love affair, and he had just won a Pulitzer Prize.
But we still found time for our talks, the turns in my life. One
night when I was brooding more than usual he took me to a jam
session of his rock band in the damp basement of a suburban
house in New Jersey. The guys strummed and fiddled, smoking
cigarettes, drinking beer. Wanting to cheer me, to include me,
Tim dragged a chair for me and, hitching up his baggy trousers,
plucked at his guitar, croaking the words to "Secret Agent Man,"
twisting and shouting, sweat soaking his shirt. I tried to join in,
but their camaraderie only made me feel lonelier, an outsider.
Quietly, wanting to shut everyone out, I went upstairs to the
library and fell asleep there on the sofa.

My birthday came, Elizabeth called, and it was then that I told
her I had not heard from the *Times* and had decided to return to
Manila to stay there until she, too, could leave. I had patched together some assignments for magazines and freelance articles for
the San Francisco paper. She listened quietly, and I expected to
hear caution on her part. She surprised me, bursting out laughing. "You crazy woman!" she said happily. She was riding high
seeing the end of our months apart and the end, too, of her long
assignment in Sri Lanka. All that time it had been strange for
me to see her byline in the paper every morning on stories she
had already told me over the phone. How different they seemed

in print—never quite as vivid in print as they seemed when she talked them out. While I was seeing the end of winter, she was up in the northeast of Sri Lanka, in Jaffna, the heart of Tamil rebel territory where the country's civil war between the Tamils and the majority Sinhalese was fought inch by inch, body by body, bombing by bombing. Her car had broken down, her driver had disappeared, and she was barely able to make it out safely. That was her life—snarled trips, unreliable drivers, military checkpoints, red tape, dead ends.

"The desk thinks I'm just here wandering around in paradise," she would say. In the last days of her assignment there, she went south to meet with rebels, drove east to the war front in Batticaloa, stopping to record the deaths—nine killed near Kantalai, nineteen dead near Potankadu, fifteen killed near Morawewa—her routes marked with a blue highlighter and the notes on the victims scribbled in black ink on a foldout map.

She ran on the beaches in Bentota, climbed the hills of tea plantations in Kandy, and jogged at sunset past the cinnamon-colored colonial buildings of Colombo, absorbed in all of it, lyrical when she wrote about it, odes to that place she strangely loved—cows on the road, elephants in her path, bombs in her hotel, smiling musicians playing only for her, the lone guest.

She returned to Manila in late April, days before my arrival. She was at the airport waiting for me, but this time she walked in a hurry, waving happily, throwing her arms around me. In the car she handed me an envelope. She had written one long passage, unsigned, recalling what she felt when she first knew me, how she thought it was her secret alone, but feared that I knew and that scared her. It was the most profound restlessness she had known, she said. That was why, she said, she never wanted us to become comfortable or routine — we were much more than that.

There they were, waiting for my arrival at the top of the stairs at P. Lovina — Edna, Gina, and Boom. In the nearly two months I had been away, Boom had ballooned, hardly recognizable as the skinny orange tabby Camilla had rescued and given to Elizabeth. Edna and Gina, wearing freshly pressed uniforms and their biggest smiles, gaped at me, still surprised that I had come back to Manila. Edna and Gina took my luggage and Elizabeth brought out wineglasses and a bottle she had saved, anticipating my return. We toasted and drank madly. At that moment, that day, everything was perfect. I was home.

No one had expected my return, but just the same everyone — Sandro and Candy, Nick, Rolly the driver, and the bellboys, waiters, and bartenders at the Manila Hotel — welcomed me back with great fanfare.

Soon it was the middle of June, and Elizabeth was flying to Vietnam, where the telephone lines did not work and the telex rarely did. She couldn't receive any mail, moving from hotel to hotel, traveling the length of the country, preparing to do a series of stories about a place that up until then had rarely let American reporters in. Without letters to write her and without our long phone calls to consume my day, I had nothing but time on my hands.

In the mornings I idled alone by the hotel pool, looking

around for familiar faces, for Leo the tennis pro, or the chatty women at the tennis club front desk, or the easygoing hotel staff that catered to my whims. Without Rolly to drive me around, because he only worked when Elizabeth needed him, I would walk two blocks from P. Lovina to Roxas Boulevard to pick up a taxi. I walked quickly past the squatter camp, which had grown to the size of a barangay, a small village of double-decker shacks, sari-sari stores, and food stands. Taxis zipped by on Roxas, filthy, without door handles, windows, or air conditioning, but with Jesus dolls hanging by a string and swinging off rearview mirrors. I would get to the hotel and have my coffee by the pool, sometimes indulging in the barrio breakfast of corned beef hash and fried eggs while swatting away the flies. There was hardly anyone around. By noon the tedium set in, and I entertained myself by looking up at the balcony of room 817, envisioning Elizabeth there, a blot of red hair at that distance, waving down at me, and I imagined returning to that room one day, in our tenth year together, and sitting with her in those lumpy brown rattan armchairs, watching the hulking freighters in the bay, the lights below, and feeling her breath of margarita salt.

Halfheartedly, I worked on a magazine piece on the Philippine military, struggling to make it pertinent to an American audience. I sent it off to a magazine I can't recall now and began another magazine piece, a profile of Cory Aquino. In no time, or because I had so much time, the project grew, became an unwieldy sprawl, untidy stacks of pages on top of my desk. Late afternoons I was still writing, cheered one day by a rare telex from Elizabeth in Hanoi.

She was coming out of Vietnam, flying to Bangkok in July

after a month of traveling the length and width of Vietnam, from Haiphong to Hue, from Danang to Nha Trang, where children pinched her skin and wanted her sunglasses, pleading at her elbow, "I will be your sister, take me with you." There was Saigon and the Cuu Long Hotel, and she was mesmerized by the city and the river, and the girls in ao dais and the Amerasian kids, and those delicious bowls of pho in the open food stands.

I flew to Bangkok to meet her, and paced for hours in the airport's reception area, not a cocktail lounge in the place, and when her flight arrived, flashing red on the electric arrivals board, I stood at the bottom of the stairs, looking up at the long line of passengers going through immigration. Her face was turned away, and she was in animated conversation with a large, burly American in a baseball cap. She was talking with her hands, with fingers pointing. I watched her stop at the immigration booth, hand over her passport, still talking to the American, and it was then, when she looked down the stairs, that she saw me and turned again to the big man and embraced him farewell and ran down the stairs, her eyes on me. She had lost fifteen pounds, but her face was shining, sunburned, and her eyes glistened with excitement.

That week in Bangkok we played tourists, walked barefoot in the gold-encrusted Temple of the Emerald Buddha, next door to the Grand Palace, gobbled up pad thai and steamed dumplings off street vendors, and went gallery shopping on Silom Road and at markets, looking for pieces of ancient art and celadon pottery and gilded Buddha images for Elizabeth's collection. The heat was scorching, the smog suffocating, but we took a narrow wooden boat down the Chao Phraya and the smelly klongs—canals—bordered by wild orchids and palm fronds, waterlogged shacks, and moss-covered boat docks. Skinny kids in sports shorts waved as our boat passed. In her shades and a military-green T-shirt, Elizabeth resembled a character out of the veldt, handsome and strong, the strain of her long journey in Vietnam easing. After the boat ride, after the late-afternoon cocktails, the evening flowed into night in the thick summer heat of the gardens of the Oriental.

August was misery. The heat, the constant rain, the moss in the closets, the flooded garden. Elizabeth finished her series on Vietnam and then, with just a day or two off, had to turn around and fly to Seoul, a four-hour trip with a stop in Taipei. She had a fever before taking off but she insisted she had to go. When she arrived that night at the Seoul Hilton, she called. She had a rash over her chest and on her stomach; her neck, her back, and her legs ached. She was so weak, she nearly passed out during an interview. She wouldn't call a doctor. Whom do you call in Seoul? The hotel can help, I said, but she didn't listen. When the rash and the ache got worse days later, she called a doctor, but he couldn't figure out what was wrong. Leave Seoul, go to Hong Kong, I suggested, figuring that Hong Kong was only two hours away and that an English-speaking doctor might be easily available there.

I took the first flight to Hong Kong out of Manila and met her at the Mandarin Oriental. She looked awful. Her face had a scary jaundiced yellow color, and there were deep purplish hollows under her eyes. Her body shook and her stomach was covered in red blotches. Her bones ached all over and she could hardly move her neck. Within minutes of checking in at the hotel, she saw a doctor. He knew it at first sight: dengue fever. He gave her a shot and ordered her to bed. We stayed inside our quiet room for a couple of days, pampered by British civility, scones at tea-time, cream and strawberries at breakfast. She began to recover; the fever went down and her humor was back, and she could get out of the room. We browsed the shops in the Prince Building near the hotel and bought a stack of Graham Greene and Somerset Maugham paperbacks, and on the day we were leaving to go back to Manila she gave me a small black velvet box holding a delicate Swiss watch I had admired in the hotel's jewelry shop. It was her way of congratulating me on the job I had been offered at the *Times*. I would start in January 1989.

When we returned to Manila, she forced herself to spend a few more days in bed, saying all along that she should be out and about and filing stories. She worried me sometimes, refusing to take a break, so careless with her body. It was around that time that her editors told her that they were naming her replacement, the reporter who would take over her job in December. Her assignment in Asia was over and done. She sank into the seat of the butaca, telephone in one hand, cigarette in the other, shaking her head at me. We had known all along that this day would come, but it was different now. Now it was a cold reality. The life of hopping on planes and covering coups and falls of governments, a life that was a constant surprise, fascinating and maddening, was slipping away from her.

She had three months left. She flew everywhere — Thailand, Singapore, Sri Lanka, down to Mindanao and up to Cagayan — cramming in as much work as she could. But it seemed her heart had left it. She worried about the future, what she might do next, and the paper wasn't telling her. I was no help, had no answers. I would be going to the *Times* in January to work on the Foreign Desk, the kind of work I had thought I had left behind me, but I figured that perhaps Elizabeth would be sent abroad again and I would go with her and finally write that book. The last months in Manila were hectic. Typhoons battered the country, a passenger boat sank in the Visayas Sea, near the central island of Cebu, and hundreds of ferry travelers drowned. It was the worst shipwreck on record anywhere. Coup rumors and intrigue swirled up again, and military-backed cults rampaged in the provinces, slaughtering villagers and leftist rebels, cutting off their heads and posing for pictures with their trophies.

And one day Edna and Gina resigned and left. We had hoped we could help them go with us to America. They had pleaded for so long. We had put Gina through secretarial school and Edna in cooking classes. We had trusted them with the house, our things, and Boom, who was Elizabeth's little passion, the way she swept him off the floor, throwing him in the air, squeezing him tight against her. But in the end, we decided we could not take the girls. We wouldn't have room for them or the money to pay them American wages. We had to give them the bad news. On a swampy Monday morning in late August, three months before our departure, Elizabeth called them to come to the porch, where we sat at her desk. They stood before us rigidly, like wayward students at the principal's office. Their eyes downcast, they waited for the blow. Gina nodded tight-lipped while Edna clutched the hem of her apron and pouted. We felt terrible, and apologized and promised to get them jobs before we left Manila. They nodded and seemed agreeable, backing away from us politely as we kept apologizing.

But the truth was that we were not entirely happy with them. During the months when we had been away from Manila, they had entertained their friends and family in our house without asking our permission and had let the place get run down. Dirt and dust had built up in corners, under carpets, and on the baseboards and bookshelves. Elizabeth took them aside and ran her fingertip on the woodwork, showing them the soot, and ordered them to clean the house from top to bottom. They had never seen her severity. She had dealt with them more than I had; she had listened to them, asked about their family up in Tarlac province, and had treated them with dignity and respect, unfailingly polite and warm. Startled by the change in her tone, they glared at her and literally fled out of the room, got their pails and brooms, and did not raise their voices for days.

But Gina left a note for us on the kitchen table. It said, *We are not machines.* The day they left, without a word to either of us, a taxi came to get them, and, carrying their bundles, they walked from their rooms in the back through the side garden. They were wearing their old clothes, their hair dirty and messy. I thought I saw a smirk on Gina's face. They did not raise their eyes to us. We pretended we didn't care, but we felt abandoned, angry, and sad. When I checked out their rooms, which we had left entirely in their hands, I couldn't bear the smell. Dirty mattresses, filthy, overflowing toilet, urine stains, trash bags on the floor. Candy, next door, who had had maids all her life, gave us a lecture. "You were never firm with them. You should've checked in on them," she said as she made a tour of their rooms. "You've got to know Filipinos. You can't give them too much freedom. Besides, you paid them too much."

For weeks we found no one to take their place. Girls from the squatter camp came and lasted a day, and our clothes piled up unwashed. I swept and Elizabeth cooked, but we could not manage the place alone. We could not understand why the maids didn't want to work for us. We knew Candy would know. She had the ear of the servants in the compound and heard their gossip. But all she would say was, "It's one of those things, nothing to worry about." We let it go at that and finally found someone to take the job. But one day, long after all that, we got the truth out of Candy. Some of those maids, she said, sucking on her cigarette, didn't want to live in our house. "Your relationship, you know." Elizabeth blushed, raising an eyebrow. I felt a hollow ache I couldn't express. Candy flicked her cigarette. I think that was the moment when I began to leave Manila.

I had finished my profile of Cory Aquino, and Elizabeth took off on her last assignment in Sri Lanka. It was November, and it seemed everyone was gone. Sitting in Elizabeth's desk chair on the porch, I watched thunderstorms move in, ominous clouds hovering so close, they seemed to brush the treetops. I would wait for the burst of hard rain to batter in through the wire screens, spatter the tile floors, splash my legs, and drench my clothes. The pungent smell of wet earth, mossy and dank, filled the air, and I felt a lassitude those last weeks that left me already yearning for all that had been mine those years.

Elizabeth came back from Sri Lanka, and we had a couple of

weeks left with nothing left to do. We lay in our room those last nights, imagined the ordinary plaster walls of American homes, walls without geckos, and the routine of office work, and getting on subways and trains, and driving down the interstate. But we could not really imagine it—nights without bamboo rustling at our windows or the rooster crowing at dawn, and the cries of *"Balut, balut."* Holding back time, and an unknown future, she would put her head on my pillow, her hand gently silencing my mouth.

The packers came, and once again our life was crammed into boxes, brown-taped, roped, and stuffed into a van and taken away to be loaded onto a freighter that would disappear in the sapphire seas of the Pacific, churning through the Panama Canal to the Caribbean, passing only miles from the island where I was born, and turning north, far north, to New York harbor.

The house was a desert, colorless now that we were leaving it. The movers left footprints on our cedar plank floors, and there were scraps of boxes and pieces of cardboard, brown wrapping paper and rolls of tape. We left behind the beds, a wicker sideboard, the white rattan sofa, but the place still looked barren. We locked the front screen door behind us and ran down the steps into the waiting car—it was Rolly seeing us off. Elizabeth carried Boom in his new travel cage. This time I did not glance back as the car pulled out. I did not wave.

We sat apart, each taking up a corner of the back seat, looking out the windows at scenes so familiar, they had become nearly invisible, but this time they were frozen frames—the squatters, the half-naked kids in the mud, the bay green-gray and flat, the colors flashing by. I heard Rolly say, "You'll be back someday.

But when you come back, this country will be nothing but garbage piles and funeral homes. Boom is so lucky. Going to America!"

At ten in the morning on December tenth, with Boom in his cage in the cargo hold of the United plane, we boarded the flight to San Francisco, and when the plane lifted off, Elizabeth pressed her face to the window and took my hand and said, "This country can break your heart."

PART III

8

NEW YORK HAD ALWAYS been a seduction. It would always be the city that stole my heart when I was fourteen, when the city seemed to rise to meet me as I peered down on it from my window seat on a Pam Am clipper. The buildings shooting into the sky seemed great monuments to me, defying gravity, beyond imagination. I was taken by the city instantly and promised myself that one day I would walk down Park Avenue and Fifth and Central Park and have exciting evenings at the theater and live in a garret in the Village, where I would write all those poems pent up inside me. But nothing like that had happened when I returned to the city when I was nineteen years old, out of college, a dreamer getting on the train in South Carolina and riding north with twenty dollars in my wallet, head in the clouds.

I had no such illusions in January 1989. With the crunch of dirty snow under our feet and icy winds tossing about us, Elizabeth and I looked for an apartment for days and wound up renting a fifth-floor walkup in the Upper West Side, near Central Park, a brownstone with foxhound pictures framed and hung on the wallpapered foyer walls, emerald-green carpets on the stairs, and carved balusters.

Our furniture came in batches, my sofa and rugs from Tim's, and, months later, the Manila shipment, which came in airtight containers unloaded at the docks and pitchforked into a six-wheeler, which brought it to our stoop, the men puffing and panting as they lifted and shouldered each piece up five flights of narrow stairs, tearing the wallpaper, nicking the plaster. We crammed it all into three cramped rooms, nearly sunless, where light filtered through a soot-smeared skylight. The windows of the living room, which was in the rear, looked out on weather-streaked faded yellow brick, the back side of a towering apartment building.

The apartment had its charms: dark hardwood floors, a red-brick fireplace that evoked nights by the hearth, floor-to-ceiling bookshelves on one wall, a Mexican tile kitchen, and a garden roof of tarpaper, potted plants, and withered vines, with deck chairs set out for alfresco twilights. I squeezed my desk against the window in the second bedroom and made room for a twin bed for guests. The windows of both bedrooms opened out on a leafy street, looking down into the French doors of a maisonette across the street and the steam pipe in the corner, which blew hard all winter.

We were jolted awake in the middle of the night by the screech and whistles of car alarms, police sirens, ambulances, and jack-hammers on Central Park West. Boom, who'd survived the trauma of traveling in a cage in a dark and cold airplane cargo hold across the Pacific, hid for days under our bed or up in the kitchen cabinets, and so we began our new life.

Elizabeth got a job with a magazine, working out of an office with her nameplate on the door and writing pieces culled from files reported by correspondents around the world. Gone were the T-shirts and bandannas, the tennis shoes and jeans. Here she had to thread into her stories the perspectives honed at the Asia Society and the Council on Foreign Relations, and by sitting in, in her best silk, on occasional boardroom breakfasts with Kissinger. It didn't surprise me that she seemed comfortable there. This was inbred in her, a social polish that came naturally. But she was only passing time, waiting to go overseas.

I was working in a pantheon. I walked by the same names I had read in the *Times* since my early days as a newsroom clerk in Columbia, South Carolina, bylines I had known at a distance for decades. Every afternoon I arrived in the newsroom on the third floor and crossed the long rust-carpeted corridor past desks piled high with books and unopened manuscripts. Heads bent over word processors—graying heads, bald heads—women in long black skirts, their hair wind-whipped, older men in suspenders and rumpled Brooks Brothers jackets. These were the legends.

They used to say that people went to the *Times* and died there. I believed it. A sunless pallor came over your face, along with creases on your forehead and a definite slouch to your shoulders. I still have the ID picture they took on my first day. There was a smooth look on my face, a genuine smile, and my hair had life to it, shiny and dark. I was just out of Manila, still tanned, still fresh-looking, allowing myself big hopes.

But right from the start, I was not what you would call a rousing success on the Foreign Desk. I didn't throw myself into that work. On the graveyard shift, I came in every midafternoon and plunked down at my assigned desk, hung my jacket on the back of my chair, and cranked down the seat, which was left too high by the tall fellow who sat there in the mornings. The top of the desk was sticky from years of spilled drinks. Copyeditors worked in a cluster of ten desks jammed together, feet away from the Foreign backfield, where assigning editors handled reporters, did the heavy lifting on stories, and made the key decisions. The Copy Desk was something else, a rung below. We were grunts in boot camp, word technicians, or lifers who had lost ambition.

Midnight, sometimes one in the morning, after the last page proofs had been checked and marked up for the last edition and the janitors were emptying the trash cans and vacuuming the carpets, I would sign off, throw out my collection of half-drunk coffee cups, and slog out of the newsroom, down the elevator to West Forty-Third Street, which was loud with the idling engines of the newspaper delivery trucks. Huddled down against the winter wind or the cloying summer heat—it did not matter which, as weather on that block always seemed the same to me, the grime unrelieved—I walked down to Eighth Avenue, by patrolmen and truckers at the deli, and hustlers in glittering wigs and beggars sprawled on garbage bags. It was a risky block then, before the regeneration of Times Square.

There were no collegial beers after work, no dive bar. Everyone scurried their separate ways to catch the subway, the last train to Westchester, the bus to Montclair or Hoboken across the river. After a few months of this tedious routine, working the night shifts and on weekends, too, my once tanned skin took on a fluorescent gray color, a sallow cast. I had pouches under my eyes, and my hair had a droopy look, flattened around an aging face.

Elizabeth had the power surge she usually experienced in new jobs. She immersed herself, and, a quick study, she was soon in command of her work. She had late Friday-night dinners with the office crowd, with bottles of fine wine. And when she was done with her day, which started at the normal hour of ten and usually finished around six, she did not have to walk down to Eighth Avenue for a cab at midnight or slide on spit on the Times Square subway stairs. Keeping in mind that I didn't have the office life she did, she would bring me leftovers from her dinners and would always wait up for me. She could hear me on the landing, shuffling up that last long flight, turning the doorknob of the apartment door, and double-locking it behind me. She waited for me to come in and, springing up from the armchair where she had been seated, already in pajamas, her hair damp from her bath, she would stand expectantly, with a hopeful smile. But she could read my mood in seconds, the way I yanked off my coat and threw it on the sofa. I would go directly to the fridge and grab a can of beer, without a touch or a smile for her.

I always sat in the narrow loveseat, and she across from me in an old armchair. We smoked a few cigarettes, talked about my day: the rejected headlines, the glacial pace, the prissy editor who carried a schedule sheet on a clipboard, assigning us work shifts, looking down on me with his lips pursed. I ranted on and on. She laughed at some of my stories but was more often pained, seeing the toll the job was taking. Night after night she would go to bed alone, but I would stay up late, having one last cigarette, one last beer, trying to figure out what was going wrong. After a while, after the first months, I had no funny stories to tell her after work. The early enthusiasm I had for my job in the first few weeks had gone. It was all showing on my face, in the stoop of my back when I walked to the subway, the life of Manhattan dead to me.

Summer, then fall 1989. I stopped smoking and stashed away the few pages of the book I had completed, shoved the pages in an envelope in the bottom of my desk drawer. "Someday you'll do it," Elizabeth said. "It's just not the right time now." But I felt hopeless, defeated, and let myself slide into the old doubts. Perhaps for that reason, I was trying harder at work to prove myself. I memorized the style book and polished my headlines and caught obscure errors in copy. I stopped glaring at the finicky editor who brought his own cloth rag to clean his screen and lived on a diet of yogurt and tofu. After a while, the eccentricities of copyeditors became normal. I didn't notice anymore the editor, already twenty years in service, who opened his large umbrella and propped it on his desk to shield him from anyone passing by. Eventually I got a turn on the backfield and I felt the lift that recognition can give, the old newspaper charge.

We saw few of our reporters, could go years without meeting them face-to-face. But on the occasions when one or another came to town on home leave, from Rio or Warsaw or Jerusalem, from any one of the forty bureaus the *Times* maintained overseas, he (almost always he) would come by to meet all of us on the desk. Courteous and dressed in fine tailored suits, the correspondents looked and behaved more like diplomats than the foreign correspondents in our crowd in Manila. Even the young who'd gotten their start on minor outposts such as the Ivory Coast and the Caribbean had their hair trimmed and their poplin jackets pressed. Nobody looked rumpled.

Every morning I took a walk up and down Columbus and Amsterdam to pick up magazines and flowers, milk or cigarettes, and I would suddenly halt, as in a fog, at the sight of a face, the thick black hair of a girl I knew immediately had to be a Filipina, round hips, pout, sweet lilt. Or sometimes, when I came out of the apartment and was struck by the evocative tropical smell of bus fumes and warm rain, I would feel it inside my body, the smell of the tropics, right there on Broadway.

Some of our friends from Manila showed up occasionally in New York, a rotation of drop-ins and overnight guests. "That's one thing about New York," Elizabeth liked to say. "Everyone comes through here."

Kay lived nearby, and saved videotapes of news programs on the Philippines, hoarded letters from friends there, and spent days in her apartment going through pictures and faxes of newspaper clippings from Manila. Camilla flew in from London, then holed up for days at the Pierre. Sandro dropped in too, looking raffish and seductive as always, smoking up New York. He seemed younger, flushed with lust for a lithe Turkish stewardess he had met on one of his flights. Things had changed in Manila, he said. He had left Candy, had closed down his house and studio, had quit the magazine job, and was planning to move to Jerusalem. Giving us a shock, he broke the news that our homes on P. Lovina were being torn down to make way for an expansion of EDSA, the expressway that had been a symbol of the People Power Revolution. His glow made my mood darken, and I bristled when he asked if I was still writing. Worse, I was sure he could sense that Elizabeth and I had strayed since the days he knew us, when we had seemed in lockstep and confident in our relationship. That evening in New York, the three of us sat in our living room for hours, rehashing our lives, and then, with lush kisses on both cheeks to each of us, crunching embraces, and an extravagant *"Ciao!,"* he was gone, leaving us with the heavy sound of his steps down the stairs.

Candy came during the Christmas holidays. She was thinner, even thinner than she had been in Manila, and was still mourning her breakup with Sandro. But she was making a valiant effort to cheer herself with a shopping spree for clothes and gifts on Madison Avenue, dinners in Greenwich Village, and plans to leave the Philippines. After the excitement on her arrival at our apartment, she cried over a glass of wine, heartbroken but hardened, and feigning optimism that she would find a way out of Manila and a new life. We caught up on gossip—we knew the same people and kept track—and her singsong voice carried Manila in it. But I noticed too that she was studying Elizabeth closely, and studying me. I saw in her eyes a flicker of concern that we seemed so different than we had been in Manila.

We were successful, true. I had a paycheck and enjoyed the status that came automatically with a job at the *Times*. But it was all a surface gloss. We were both unhappy doing office work and feeling trapped and at the same time displaced or suspended, somehow out of step. We were marking time until we could leave New York. Around that time, Nick came to town. We had dinner, drinks. He was dashing as always, sun-bleached, tousle-headed in his safari shirt, downing Dos Equis at a Mexican restaurant a few blocks from our apartment. He was on his way back to India. "What are you doing sitting in an office on Madison Avenue?" he asked Elizabeth, needling her. He could always get to her, knew her soft spots, and I could see her jaw clamping. She grabbed his cigarettes and took a swig of beer.

"I'm taking a break." She said she was tired of the road and was expanding her understanding of foreign policy. "You know, waiting for an assignment." He twirled his mustache, looking skeptical. He had a few wrinkles around his brow, baggy eyes, some gray facial hair, but the years didn't show on him. He swore that he kept trim and fit by drinking beer. He was the old Nick, filling us in on his latest escapade, an overland trip to Kabul, dodging bombs and bullets, and on the Manila gossip, on how the place had gone to hell since we had left. We liked to believe that Manila could not possibly be the same without us.

That year Elizabeth bought a country house on a creek upstate, a few miles down the road from a tumbledown town with a lone fire truck and a general store where the supplies gathered dust on shelves and the screen door banged loose in the breeze. The house, a fieldstone gray-clapboard with big windows, had a fruit orchard and herb garden, and a canopy of birch and oak trees.

Here was a refuge from the city. When our schedules worked out, we drove up with Boom, Elizabeth chattering the second we left Manhattan behind. She could make the drive in two hours flat, a Big Mac on her lap, the tape player blasting. Arriving at our house—after the turnoff from the main highway and the stretch on a hilly rural moonlit road—was always an event. Deer on the road, crickets singing, the rustle of corn stalks, the silhouette of an old farmhouse across the road.

While I loved big-city life, Elizabeth chafed against living within four walls, in a walkup apartment or a row house, squeezed between one building and another, within earshot of neighbors, without a plot of land to trowel. She wasn't a window-box gardener, one of those city people who could turn a rooftop into a greenhouse. She wanted soil under her nails, something loamy to sink her feet into. Her face would light up at a clump of fresh rosemary, and the office stress would ease the minute she spotted mallards on the creek, and geese scampering out of the woods. A shock of hair flopping on her high forehead and with her back muscles loosened, she could look twelve years old.

The house brought us respite, the strain that had grown between us lessening. I could forget for a while the aggravations of work, the dreary six-to-one night shift and the wasted mornings and afternoons I spent alone in the apartment as I waited impatiently for late afternoon to come, when Elizabeth would finish work and walk across Central Park on the way home. Sometimes I would meet her midway, watching her figure from a distance; I watched the quickness or slowness in her step, the way she lugged her leather bag, the angle of her head, and could guess how her day had gone. Then we would walk together to the apartment, had long enough for a few words and a light touch, and I would leave for work.

The country house restored some of the serenity and companionship we missed in New York. I didn't turn away from her when she threw her arms around me, and I didn't quarrel over every little slight. Relaxed on a deck chair, my feet on the railing, the sun on my face, I could even believe writing was possible again. We planted a pear tree to leave our mark there and weeded the orchard and Elizabeth groomed the herb garden and planted daffodil bulbs for spring. She had tree limbs trimmed back and a sturdy dock built into the creek. We bought a sofa and armchairs and furnished the rest with pieces we couldn't fit in the New York apartment. We unpacked books that had been boxed for years and bought a red Maine canoe. She tried to teach me to paddle and to cast and reel on slow afternoons in the creek when we were the only people around. Nights drew down slowly, with long talks before the fire and wine. I would wake up early in our cedar-wood bedroom to find that she was already up, standing stock-still on the sun deck, her binoculars pressed to her face.

"Come here. Look," she would call out to me. "Did you see that? A blue heron."

The muscles in her face strained instantly when we crossed back to the city, the traffic jam boiling her temper. "I hate this city," she said every time. I knew what she meant. We had let the world dictate our life, the world of nine-to-five and superficial distractions and old complications. But that was not all. Out of the blue, Elizabeth's work took an unexpected turn that spring when an editor approached her and, under the guise of concern, told her things he had heard about me and her, such a strange relationship. Her heart was still pounding and her hands clammy when she told me about it later that day. She was indignant and hurt, and in the heat of anger threatened to quit her job. I was furious too, but office rumors, those little scandals, were all too familiar to me. I had lived through many years of that. For Elizabeth, it was a shock. I never saw it coming, she said. But it was something she had feared, having our private life vulgarized. Over the next days and weeks, she put on a good face at work, and the editor who had crossed the line apologized. Elizabeth didn't quit. But she couldn't feel totally at ease at work anymore, and we didn't know if after all that she would still get a foreign assignment.

The waiting seemed endless, and we didn't exactly agree on where we wanted to go. I wanted to go back to Asia—New Delhi, Bangkok, Hong Kong. She wanted South Africa or even Latin America, though she didn't mind returning to Asia at all. Now and then I turned my frustration with work and myself against her, unleashing the familiar but still stinging words that I knew wounded her, and she responded in the familiar and biting way. Taut jaw, high chin, firing eyes, she bristled at the old litany I dragged out—that she had had it all, she was cold and distant, she came easily to success.

"Why don't you leave if you feel like that," she burst out one night, words she had thrown at me during one of our fights in

Manila. She grabbed her field jacket and left the room, slamming the door behind her. She walked around and sat on the steps of a church near the corner, where I found her. What created this desolation? Why did I push her away? It was not lack of love. It was a fear growing in me that our life was changing, that something—I didn't know or didn't want to know exactly what—was pulling us apart. We were becoming ordinary. We no longer had the romance and excitement of Manila as our backdrop; now we had mundane jobs, nine-to-five lives. I made things worse, questioning myself, everything I had done and not done. I had wasted years, years when I didn't write, years before I met Elizabeth. Writing and my hope to make a living at it seemed a delusion.

I cried so often that year in New York, cried at night, on the sofa, walking the streets, in the subway, and woke with sickening anxiety every morning. When she wanted to hold me, I would turn away, my ardor now barely a flicker. We lay in our bed apart, each lost. "It's only a phase," she would often say, always tender, a light hand on me, about the many times when I would read a book, my back to her, when I would pull away from her and merely brush her cheek to say good night.

"It's Tokyo." She had called up to tell me her new assignment. There was such dismay in her voice. No exclamation point. I could not believe it—Tokyo? Japan was another planet, a place I had never thought of visiting, a place she knew from art and books—but it was not what we had in mind. We had wanted tropical islands and hot cities, the South China Sea, Bangkok, Jakarta. Not this, not Tokyo. She used to say she hated first world countries. Even Hong Kong was too modern for her, and now she was going to Tokyo. An editor had handed her a slip of paper with a single word on it, and an exclamation point: *Tokyo!*

I had nagged her to get out of New York, to return to Asia. And here it was; it was Asia, but not the Asia I had in mind. I felt guilty sensing her disappointment, knowing I was responsible. I tried to paint seductive pictures of life in Japan, the excitement of such an exceptional and ancient culture, the challenge it presented. "It's a big story," I offered, and I was right about that. "It's a country people here take seriously." I was also trying to convince myself while at the same time figuring out what in the world I would do there. There was little question that I would leave the *Times*. I couldn't see life without Elizabeth, and if I stayed I would be bound to desk work for the rest of my life. Now I had a reason to get out.

An assignment to Japan was not a simple matter of passport and plane ticket. It required elaborate visa applications, sponsors, and letters, and she had to spend months studying Japanese. Leaving the paper was not as easy as I had supposed. My editor's face fell when I told him behind closed doors. In the next few weeks, as word got around, other editors came by, bending down, whispering, "Is there anything we can do to keep you?" On my last week at the paper—I had been there only eighteen months—the desk surprised me with chilled bottles of Taittinger and a cake, and a round of farewell speeches. On another day that week, the foreign editor and the managing editor hosted a lunch for me in a private dining room in the upper floor of the newspaper tower. There were waiters in uniform, Bloody

Marys, wine, a lavish lunch, toasts, and gifts—a pen set I long ago lost somewhere and the navy blue duffel that still travels with me.

We still had some time before leaving for Japan. I got a journalist visa, arranged to do stories out of Tokyo and Southeast Asia for the *San Francisco Chronicle*, and went back to the book I had started in Manila. But suddenly, it seemed, Elizabeth was gone—but not to Japan. She was in the Persian Gulf. Saddam Hussein had invaded Kuwait, and the United States was going to war. We were sitting in our living room when she got the call from her editors. They were sending her and other correspondents to the Gulf on a military plane. She had less than twelve hours to get ready. She flinched but knew she wanted to go; this was what she loved doing. Hovering at her side while she was still on the phone, I nodded yes, go.

It was January 1991, more than two years since she had last climbed onto a plane and landed continents or oceans away in a country she didn't know. Few things were more daring and exciting in the business than landing in—parachuting into—a foreign country. She could not turn down the chance to cover a war. Being chosen for that assignment was a clear statement that she was on her way up. Over the years I had grown accustomed to her absences, but something gnawed at me, something she had said days before that phone call. "I have a feeling something big is going to happen," she had said, "something that will change everything."

She left the night the war began, on January sixteenth. Around midnight, after the bombing of Baghdad had begun and President Bush had gone on television to speak to the nation and we had dashed around town buying desert gear for her. I watched her go, and guessed she was a little scared and already lonely.

She wrote me days after her arrival in Dhahran, off the Persian Gulf. She and a team of other correspondents and photographers were booked in a hotel, doing nothing, waiting for something to happen. Everyone was tense, she said, and so was she, feeling off-stride, disoriented, at loose ends.

Between her occasional calls and letters, I was writing again. It had been a long time. Every noon I walked to the corner deli for a sandwich, and in the mornings I walked down Columbus Avenue, the mist-clouded tips of the Midtown skyscrapers on the horizon, to pick up out-of-town newspapers. I passed by a scruffy plaza on Sixty-Fifth Street where immigrant laborers gathered, stocky Salvadoran men in Yankees windbreakers, playing dominoes and tossing beer bottles. They rarely raised their eyes to me, or I to them, but I would slow down, catching the music in their boom boxes, music I used to hear at night when I was a child trying to sleep, boleros that drifted in through my bedroom window.

I saw no friends for weeks on end, but CNN kept me entertained. I searched for Elizabeth's face at news conferences televised in Dhahran and Riyadh; and sometimes, when I was working in my study, I would overhear her voice on television, maybe a question she was posing to the colonel debriefing the media, and I would rush to the living room to watch her, as if she were speaking directly to me. I could almost clock her day, knew that when it was evening in the desert, she would call. Often I fell asleep on the sofa, a blanket over me, Boom at my feet,

the TV still on, and then the phone would ring, her voice so
near.

This was a hotel war, she complained, a television war, a war
by press conference, briefings, and canned interviews. On top
of that, there was nothing to drink, no gin, no wine, no Scotch.
After the tense days of lethargy in Dhahran, where the media
was herded around and corralled in hotel suites, she bolted, took
a jeep across the desert and arrived in Riyadh, where she thought
she might have a freer hand, could interview top generals and
Saudi princes and sneak out on nighttime rides into the military
camps.

She was much more chipper then, burying herself in work.
But some days she felt at a loss, suspended, waiting for the war,
waiting to go home. It seemed she had been gone a long time,
but it had been only a month or so. Loneliness was the theme
of those letters, what she called mumblings in the desert. I put
up the photos and postcards she mailed me—attack helicopters,
Arabs in burnooses, a Saudi flag and a war decal, and her drawings, one a picture of her in the dunes, a redheaded stick figure
overshadowed by the vastness of the desert, empty but for the
outline of a lone camel.

On the day of her return from the Gulf I rose before dawn,
got dressed, and took a taxi to JFK. I got there early, with time to
smoke and drink a beer and flip through a couple of magazines.
I could not sit still. Finally, the plane landed. She came out of the
terminal pushing the luggage cart, in her khakis and Timberland
boots, her face lush, her hair held up with a barrette.

She filled our room with tulips, raspberries and cream, and
Moët et Chandon, and she gave me a pair of fine gold bracelets

she had bought in the Riyadh gold souk and elegant Guerlain candles she had found in Paris. It had been two months — we felt every hour of that separation, could feel it in our touch.

She looked delicate that evening in her gray wool skirt and a charcoal cashmere jacket with black velvet lapels. Her white silk blouse was buttoned up to her neck, a graceful touch. She was dressed for a banquet her bosses were hosting to celebrate the magazine's coverage of the war. With a dab of Chanel No. 19 on the nape of her neck, and black suede slippers on her feet, she walked to the dinner alone, her arms folded self-consciously across her chest as if to hide herself from the world, not knowing the sight she made, how she stopped my heart.

In Manila I came to believe that places can change you, can give life or take it away. Manila had been life to us, a birth, the beginning of a time that we could not possibly have imagined.

But Japan was deadening.

Three months in Tokyo, and I watched her withering, a gloom that perhaps was too deep for tears. We had something of a life, I suppose. We tried to accommodate that odd city, a style of life that was not us at all, in a country of rigid faces and stifling manners. We bought Japanese objects for our apartment, a large three-bedroom ground-floor space that didn't get much light in Shoto, an expensive neighborhood where *gaijin* were allowed to live (the broker only showed us apartments she deemed suited for American and European tastes — large, carpeted, modern). We learned to slurp our noodles like the Japanese do and ventured into the *izkaya*, where drinkers gaped at us, female foreigners, and the manager would not let us in. It took us a while to sort out the unspoken rules, the mazelike neighborhoods, the giant stores, and find our way around an incredibly difficult city to navigate where homes have no numbers and streets no names—and very few people speak English.

I worked at my writing for days without seeing the sky, shut in the flat except for my walks to the 7-Eleven where I bought Sapporo beer and the clerks snickered when my back was turned. Some days, when I was desperate for any voices, I walked down to a department store in Shibuya, one of the city's busiest districts, and stood in line at the bakery, bowing to the girl, who, even after months of seeing me almost every week, did not show a trace of recognition.

Even so, it was easier for me than it was for Elizabeth. I didn't have to leave the house, could plop down for hours in front of the TV watching CNN International. Elizabeth had to show up every weekday at the magazine's offices in the Ginza, dressed in appropriate business attire, feigning a studious interest in her work, looking for the twist that might make a story compelling. She left the house in the mornings already dreading her day, and walked down narrow streets to the Shibuya subway station. Sometimes I walked with her and saw her off at the stairs to the train platform, her auburn head disappearing quickly into the crowd of white shirts, black ties, and dark heads.

These were not bandanna days. Tokyo was a business story, she would say. It was not a war, not a coup, not an uprising, nothing crazy and unexpected about it. She felt out of her element. Covering Tokyo was a straitjacket for her. How did she end up among the pinstriped men and bow-tied women of the Tokyo foreign press?

There was still a profound closeness about us, what kept us, I think, afloat. Our affection, now ingrained, showed in the small things. She still called out for me when she got home, and I always ran to the door, and we walked arm in arm to the sofa. Sometimes, often, I couldn't wait for her arrival and would meet her at the subway stairs and we would stroll home, immersed in ourselves in the crowds of those streets, feeling as alone as we had ever felt anywhere. She would say later that I had saved her. But I wonder now about the nights that faded into days, all too much the same, when I was racked with self-doubt, and those moments that left us lonely, the loneliness that comes when you have known total communion and then feel its absence. Yet her touch was like air to me, essential to my life. No one else, nothing else, could bring me the total joy her eyes did, her laughter, her being. But I was too much consumed by uncertainty and drifted away into writing and books, and she, unable to sleep, would leave our room and sit up for hours on the sofa, Boom on her lap, her nails chewed. I found escape in Manila. The flight from Tokyo was only four hours, a hop after the two-hour bus ride from central Tokyo to Narita airport. On a trip to Manila the summer of 1991, I found out that Imelda Marcos was planning to return to the Philippines after six years in exile in Hawaii and New York. At the time, Imelda was living in Manhattan, plotting her homecoming, a carnival that had Manila all excited. I thought that the return of Imelda to Manila, against the background of the end of the presidential term of Cory Aquino, could stir up some interest in the American media. I worked on a one-page story proposal and Elizabeth loved it and thought I should fax it to magazines in New York to see if I could get an assignment.

On a whim, I faxed it to *Vanity Fair*. I didn't know anyone at the magazine and chose an editor's name at random from the grouping on the magazine's masthead. Within two days, I got a call. It was one in the morning in Tokyo, and on the phone was *Vanity Fair*. Standing because I was too nervous to sit, clutching the telephone and listening to the editor on the other end, I mouthed the news to Elizabeth. Afterward, at that hour of night, we walked to the all-night 7-Eleven and bought a bottle of wine.

In the fall of 1991 I was flying all over the place — from Tokyo to New York to Honolulu to Manila for the story on Imelda. In the Philippines, I booked Elizabeth's old room at the Manila Hotel, started smoking again, and before I knew it had fallen into the swing of the city and reporting. It was already November and I had spent weeks away from Elizabeth. Back in Tokyo, I noticed immediately that she was thinner yet, her face drawn. But she had friends and had begun to have a social life while I was gone. I got busy writing the magazine story and, incredibly, forgot her birthday. It struck her hard that she had to remind me, I could see that plainly. I had been so involved with my travel and stories and writing that I had forgotten her. Nothing I could do or say would make up for that, not for days and weeks.

We wanted to have Christmas in Manila, and when our plane landed and she looked out to those shacks and brackish water, all that was so familiar, she began to cry, recovering at last something long gone from her. "Miss Whitney! Miss Whitney!" they sang out to her at the Manila Hotel, instantly recognizing her as if she had only been away a few months, and there she was, in no time at all, laughing and sweating on the tennis courts and drinking at the Lobby Lounge. During New Year's week she was running down the beach at a private resort that Candy's family had in Mamburao, swatting mosquitoes and snorkeling for coral, and every day we had margaritas and mangoes on the sands of the South China Sea.

We entered 1992, and she was back in Tokyo but I was still in Manila, still working on the story on Imelda, covering her wacky presidential campaign. Elizabeth had said it would take me six years to make a start, and so it had. But my start meant that she was living alone in Tokyo. She had promised herself that we would leave Japan before the spring, and while I was in the Philippines, she made a quick trip to Los Angeles and New York to look for another job. Shortly after her return to Tokyo, she got a call from New York. She rang me up immediately in Manila. I was tinkering with my Imelda story, giving it one final look. I picked up the phone and heard the snap in her voice, a crackling of excitement. I leaped up from the desk and shouted from the balcony, couldn't scream enough, I was so happy.

We were leaving Japan less than nine months after we had arrived, and she had a new job. I finished my story and returned to Tokyo to join her. We drank plenty of champagne those last nights in Tokyo. Soon the movers came and we closed down the apartment, shutting the flint-gray door behind us. In our years together our life had been an endless caravan, a series of way stations, without a mapped course, without markers. We had lived on two continents, in three countries, four cities, six homes in less than eight years. We had no roots, no base but ourselves; that had been our home. All along I believed that the hard times, the tense days and angry moments—all the turbulence of our years together—could never destroy the passion that held us together, not ever, and not now.

9

THE CITY WAS exhilarating that spring of 1992, the way I had always dreamed. We had evenings over drinks in the babble of bars; Elizabeth was a comet, springing high, and we had weekends tracking down the streets of SoHo, imagining life in artists' lofts, everything in black and white. I enjoyed long lunches of pinot grigio and sashimi with glamorous editors talking up my next assignment for *Vanity Fair*, now that my name was showcased in a famous magazine stacked in supermarket racks and displayed at newsstands across the city and the nation.

Broadway was directly beneath us, the *Les Misérables* billboard sixteen floors below, across Seventh Avenue. We were staying in a hotel apartment in Midtown, a one-bedroom suite of utilitarian motel decor, hard sofas, chrome chairs, and fake ferns in cracked plastic pots. It took us weeks to get rid of the residue of the trail of people who had passed through there, the stains on the bed, the musk of cheap dressers. We had thought we would be there but a few months while we looked for a place of our own, and we did look, west and east, in Greenwich Village and SoHo, from the day we arrived in March, foggy from crossing thirteen time zones and cultures.

We wanted to find a place, get settled with our own things. But nothing we saw seemed right: too expensive, too small, too dark and rundown. We were not weighing the merits of this place against that place, not just that. We were trying to see our life beyond. For me, New York was the one place where I could invent and reinvent myself, infinitely lonely and then not lonely at all. But Elizabeth had other ideas. She would wake up in the middle of the night, worried, anxious. So much had changed in our lives in such a short time, and she sensed that change would come again. She couldn't see herself rooted in New York for years, on those crowded streets, sitting on a stoop to see the moon in starless skies. It wasn't her kind of place, but I refused to see it her way.

All the while, between March and November 1992, she traveled from one city to another doing stories, from Buffalo to Miami, from feminist protests to hurricanes, and I flew on assignments to Tokyo and Rio de Janeiro. Between flights and hotels, we lived the New York life, rushed hellos and goodbyes, burnished nights on the town, rambling conversations during which we followed a bottle of wine with Armagnac.

But the strain was there. We were living whole lives apart. She was alone much of the time, most of that summer and fall, all that time to herself in that stifling, boxy flat on Seventh Avenue. This time our separations did not bring us closer. I was not in every sliver of her stories. I was not in every sinew. Those days when every letter and phone call bound us together—from Manila, from Sri Lanka, from Seoul—were gone. We didn't stay on the phone for hours, and we didn't write each other long, moody letters. Our phone calls, cheery and crisp, were filled with news but little sentiment, and she would often cut them short with a quick goodbye.

It took me a while to notice, but Elizabeth was drawing a circle of her own. These were new people she'd meet here and there, at work, on assignments, up and down the East Coast. She talked about them with unusual enthusiasm, with rare excitement. Anyone could see she was pulling away from me, her attention turning somewhere else. But I didn't want to see this then. I was fooling myself, swept up and blinded by the gloss of magazine life, drinks at the Pierre, all-afternoon lunches at the Royalton, dinners with pumped-up, blasé writers in love with themselves, their names and faces recognized in fancy restaurants and hot bars.

A few times I dragged Elizabeth into these scenes. I wanted people to meet her, wanted to share that world with her. But this was exactly the sort of scene she detested, and I knew that but it didn't stop me. I pleaded until she finally would agree to join me. She would cringe in silence while watching me, with too many glasses of wine, take over the room, sometimes arguing or ranting about one or another issue, and, worse, going out of control, cutting someone down with a sharp remark. Strung out, I knew she was watching me. I was a stranger to her at that moment. She couldn't say anything directly to me, could only avert her eyes and pretend she wasn't paying attention. At the end of those evenings, when they went badly, when I had drunk too much and found myself isolated from the rest of the guests, she would walk home paces ahead of me, silently, the depth of our break in every stride, in the way she jerked away from me.

Odd, how cycles are broken. From the beginning, writing had drawn us together, our dreams of it, our passion for it. Writing was paramount, a thread coiled around us and stretched over distances. I often thought that sharing that work, even the shallows of it, those torments of self-doubt, was perhaps the ultimate connection of our lives. Yet that year in New York, when we spread apart and she was forging a new path and I was dashing from one magazine article to another, the binding began to break. We did not care less, but we had less and less time to read over each other's shoulders and to call up with a phrase or an idea as we had during our time in Manila and the other places of our early years. We now had other editors, encouragement elsewhere.

Slowly, maybe too slowly, Elizabeth relied on me less and less. She didn't ask me to read her articles before she filed them, and she stopped asking me for advice. Occasionally I would read her a passage of mine, and she would listen attentively but with a reserve. "You may be the real writer in this family," she said, lavishing praise, but I felt she was holding back.

For so long she had allowed me to push her in one direction or another out of a notion she had that I was wiser, that I moved faster than she did. Impatiently, often with no care for her own choices, I pushed my view of things on her, my sense of what was right for her and what was not. Now a bitter resentment that had festered since Manila was coming out of her. She was no longer listening to me. There was something else I couldn't figure out, something that weighed on her.

Yet on the surface those were good days for her. She was covering stories she cared about, rushing off to report on protests, disasters, and tragedies, hopping on two-engine planes and landing in wrecked American cities, a foreign correspondent in her own country. She came alive on the road. I could always picture her so easily when she was away. There she was in the industrial debris of Buffalo, tracking anti-abortion protests, wearing her drab olive pea coat, a black fountain pen clenched between her teeth while her notebook got soaked in the rain. I was in New York, finishing a story on Tokyo's closed society, one of those quick in-and-out assignments that seemed all glamour but were in fact exhausting. I was finishing the story that day, the twenty-first of August, our sixth anniversary, and the flowers I ordered had just been delivered to a hotel in Coconut Grove where she was staying when she called up to tell me they were evacuating the hotel ahead of the landing of Hurricane Andrew, which was headed toward Miami. She didn't know where she would spend the night. I was frantic, but she was eerily calm, the way she got when something seriously bad had happened. She found a place to stay and filed stories of floods and homes destroyed over the next few days. When I asked her about the anniversary flowers I had sent her, she said quite casually that she'd had to leave them behind in the hotel when they were evacuated. It made sense, but picturing those flowers in an empty room stung me beyond reason.

She was still in Florida when I got a new assignment. I was

going to Rio de Janeiro, and I had to leave quickly. "What a life you lead!" she exclaimed on the phone, and within days she was back in New York and we celebrated at our regular place on West Fifty-First Street, where the waiters topped our wineglasses before we emptied them. We had only a few days left together, Labor Day weekend, before I was taking off for Brazil. Despite the rush of those days, we finally found a place we really liked, near the Museum of Natural History. It was a turn-of-the-century brownstone with twelve-foot ceilings, shuttered windows, sunsplashed rooms, buffed dark wooden floors, working fireplaces, and a walled-in brick garden out back. It would not be available for months, not until December. But it was breathtaking—and it was exorbitant. We sat for a long time on the staircase landing, looking out on the garden and the grand living room with its fine wainscot paneling, contemplating what life might be like in that house, how wonderful it would be, cloistered from the car horns, sirens, and dirty smells of Midtown where we had spent nine months in that sad hotel apartment. I knew we had to take the brownstone. It was the home we both wanted. We needed it to survive.

I arrived in Rio with a handful of out-of-date telephone numbers and no personal connections, and then there was the fact that I spoke no Portuguese. Elizabeth used to say that when she was on assignment, she lived in fear. In Rio I really understood what she meant. Thrust into an unfamiliar situation, with hundreds of reporters buzzing around and editors watching from afar, matching my story against those of the competition, I felt my throat tightening with a nauseating fear that I would come up

dry. Panic attacks, coughing spells, dizziness, or all were part of
the work, and they had a way of coming up at crucial moments,
in the middle of an interview, at a formal dinner, during an intro-
duction to a head of state.

My assignment was simple and direct: to get the first interview
with President Fernando Collor de Mello, who was in seclusion
during impeachment proceedings on charges of corruption.
With his high-society, playboy image, he was a big draw, and
the story of his downfall was making the front pages around the
world. But he was giving no interviews, which meant that two
hundred, maybe a thousand of us in the media were left nibbling
on the edges of the story. I stayed awake through the eight-hour
overnight flight from JFK, determined to be the one reporter
to break through, worried that another magazine would get the
interview first. That would kill mine.

A week in Rio, and I was moving into the society of characters and wealthy grandes dames of Collor de Mello's world, absorbed in lurid tales of his sexual life and greed and the dark secrets of the prominent Collor family. I had filled three notebooks
and a handful of tape cassettes in three weeks, had taught myself
some Portuguese by reading half a dozen newspapers every day,
and flew to Brasília to get a look at the political circus: the impeachment proceedings against Collor.

Brasília may be the only boring place in all Brazil, but in those
days, in the fall of 1992, it was a carnival. Tens of thousands of
anti-Collor activists took over the wide avenues of the capital,
lying about and sleeping on the green lawns of the magnificent
center of government, in front of the starkly austere house of
Congress, and in the lobbies of Brasília's hotels. When the pro-

tests and the speeches inside the Congress were over, I flew in a thunderstorm back to Rio and began to write my story. I had five days to finish it and meet the magazine's deadline. By now I had become a fixture at the Caesar Park Hotel overlooking Ipanema beach, and had my banquette at the bar and my six o'clock gin and tonic. Clerks, waiters, and housekeepers looked after me, sending up fresh-cut flowers and platters of papaya, chiding me because I was too thin and pale, working too hard, battened down in my room, writing.

Elizabeth and I talked often, her voice always surprising me. For weeks she was patient, curious about the story, wanting to know everything about Rio and the people I was meeting and those nights on the town that fizzled out around three in the morning. But by my sixth week in Brazil, a period that turned out to be much longer than I had expected when I took on the assignment, she sounded chillingly lonely and remote.

Some days I had to take a break from writing and get out of my room. I strolled down the Rua Baráo da Torre a few blocks away, and walked lazily by the Banana Café and the Hippopotamus Club, where I had gone to a flashy party one night, and peeked in fancy boutiques and stopped by the side of vendors, tempted by the smoky food. I was swinging along to the bossa nova of the streets, inhaling the smell of the tropics again, and I would think back to Manila, and how I had felt there. Rio was not the same. Rio did not have the equatorial heat of Manila, the pungent aromas, the tall palm trees. Rio did not have Elizabeth.

The October air was crisp and sharp in New York the day I returned from Rio. I had been away seven weeks. It had been so long that Elizabeth came to the airport to welcome me home, a

long drive from Manhattan to Kennedy. I was so surprised to
see her there that I stopped walking on the spot, transfixed. She
was standing inches apart from everyone else, her hair ruffled
over the upturned collar of her brown suede coat, her sunglasses
pushed up on her head, her right arm pressed across her midriff,
her face serene. I felt all the distance vanishing, and the rift of
our last six months closing. I wanted her desperately, wanted to
keep her there, with me.

Putting her hand on my elbow, her eyes softly on me, she said
happily, knowing she would surprise me, "I have a car waiting!"
It was her way of welcoming me back, to make a special gesture,
and when we arrived home, still at the hotel apartment, I flung
my bags in the hallway and threw my arms around her. She held
me, but I sensed restraint, something I couldn't read flickering in
her eyes. She went on to work right away, and that evening we
went out, sat at a small table by a window away from the jangle
of the restaurant crowd. I was bone-tired but exuberant, splashing wine into her glass, touching her hand. It had been so long.

The next day I walked to Fifth Avenue and pushed through
the glass doors of Cartier's, peered into the glittering display
cases, tiptoeing in the funereal hush of the store. After a while I
saw what I wanted. That evening when she opened the red and
gold box, she took a deep breath and looked at it for a long time.
My eyes were on her, anxious, waiting. She took the heavy gold
ring and placed it in the palm of her hand and raised her eyes to
me, her face a deep pink, and she slid the ring against the other
one I had once given her in Manila, on the second finger of her
left hand.

Two weeks later, on the day after President Clinton's election, when I was unwinding, knowing that my Brazil story was scheduled to come out in the next issue of the magazine, my editor there called. He had heard that the *New York Times Magazine* was coming out with a cover article on Collor de Mello that Sunday. He sounded tense and annoyed. My mind scrambled, my heart thumped. I knew my story was dead. We could not be seen as trailing the *Times*. This was exactly what I had feared. I called Elizabeth, told her my story was dead. It was my fault—that's all I could think of. She tried to sympathize, but I wouldn't listen and hung up. "This happens all the time," an editor friend at the magazine assured me, shuffling papers on her desk while keeping an eye on me. I kept pacing, smoking, speaking loudly, making quite a spectacle of myself in her office. Fuming, striking out at everyone but especially myself, I left her office and walked into a lashing rainstorm, one of those hellish downpours in which umbrellas turn inside out and people hang on to the side of buildings, mashed like fallen leaves by the wind that rails on the city. I was drenched. By the time Elizabeth got home I had been lying on the couch for a couple of hours, staring out the living room windows into the flashes of lightning in the black sky, running my hand on Boom's furry back, the softest surface around.

She came in quietly carrying a dozen red roses and placed them—the only bright color in the room—in a glass on top of the television set. I looked up, without a smile, and mumbled thanks and flopped back into a dead stare, a familiar downward spiral. She sat across from me, not near enough to touch me, and tried to reassure me. "It is not your fault. You had a great story." But I was intransigent, and juvenile, saying nothing, looking away from her. Finally, exasperated, she pleaded, "What do you want from me?"

With that she left the apartment for a cocktail party. I stayed on the couch all night, in the jeans and shirt I had worn all day. "You don't get it," she blurted out the next morning. "You still don't understand what you do to me, to yourself." She was disconsolate; my apologies, too late, too lame, were flicked away with a cold shrug. Too quickly she was gone to work. She walked down Broadway, her eyes fixed on the sidewalk, a wispy figure disappearing into the mob in Times Square, so invisible that, like anyone else in New York City, she could cry and no one would notice.

Incredibly, I had to go back to Brazil. The interview with President Collor de Mello came through, finally. Overnight I was on my way to Rio. I would wait days in Rio for word that the president would see me in his villa in Brasília. It was during that wait in my hotel room in Rio, late in the afternoon, talking to Elizabeth on the phone, when I heard in her voice the ice burn I knew too well. Still smoldering from those last awful nights in New York, she was curt, impersonal. For the first time in all our years, the warmth in her seemed entirely gone. She was saying the words I had dreaded.

"We need to talk when you get back."

Her tone gave me no hope. I stared at the walls of my room, and her voice seemed very far. I felt myself sinking and my hands started to shake. My voice dropped, a quiver. I didn't eat or sleep that night or the next or the next, and three days after that call, after I had finished the interviews I had to do, I took the first plane to New York. She was not at the airport, and I took a taxi into Manhattan. The city was just emerging from the early-morning haze, the sky a lavender bruise. She was waiting in the apartment, seated on the edge of the sofa, looking down on the scuffed carpet. She had been crying, I could see the red-rimmed eyes, and not daring to touch her, I took a chair, my hands trembling when I lit her cigarette. We sat looking at each other and away from each other for what seemed a long time. "If you don't change," she said slowly, each word stinging like a hard slap to the face, "I will leave you." I cannot remember if I said anything or made a noise, but I remember that I had to gulp back tears but they rolled down my face, down my chin, and onto my lap.

She was tired of our fights, my moods and depressions. "I can't rescue you anymore." That was not all. She felt I was choking her, stifling her. She winced, saying she no longer felt safe with me. She was groping for words, her head lowered, her voice grave. I nodded but had no response. My ears were roaring from the blood rising to my head. I could not hear her words but felt each of them. I don't know if I spoke—surely I did—but I knew I couldn't defend myself. I had run out of things to say.

We know how passion disintegrates. There are thin cracks, coded words. A distance that we cannot quite measure grows silently, steadily. Sometimes, too often, it happens when we are most comfortable, when life becomes routine, and the touch that once burned no longer stirs our blood. I have had loves that died when I wasn't looking, when I had forgotten, when the love became something I had misplaced.

That is not what came to us.

Our life had its own wild rhythm, unchoreographed, uncharted. We moved into our new brownstone the day before New Year's Eve, finally ending nine months of waiting to have a permanent home and have our furniture and pictures and books with us again. But nothing was quite the same. I was worn out from work, from travel, from the fear that our relationship was so frayed and tenuous that it could snap in an instant. The Christmas holidays gave us no comfort, and no time. All the recognition I had received, whatever success, had cost me — had cost both of us.

Without even a day to get us settled in our apartment, I had to fly out on a last-minute assignment to Florida and do a story on a Cuban defector that didn't interest me much but mattered to the magazine. I was leaving Elizabeth with all the annoying irritations of moving, alone in that large place, boxes still unpacked. I left at dawn on New Year's Day, 1993. She saw me off from the front window, Boom in her arms. Throwing my bag in the back seat, I had the wrenching sensation of loss, and the trip was miserable.

There were weeks in January and February when I was away most of the time, working, spending agonizing hours in hotel rooms, Elizabeth's voice on the phone no longer my tether to the world. In between we had moments of peace when life seemed to recover a semblance of joy, when we strolled up Amsterdam Avenue and drank copious amounts of wine at Louie's Westside Café, where they saved a back table for us and left us alone but overheard everything.

"You are changing," she said approvingly, grateful that I wasn't pushing her or poking at her to analyze what had gone wrong. I seized on those encouraging words, lighting up, and we walked home arm in arm. I had been trying to change, appeasing her, minding every word I said, going to therapy to sort out my head. It was an irony that just as we were breaking apart, we were at the same time more open about our relationship. But I could not tamp down the sorrow threading through it all, fearing that it was already too late to change anything, that she was smoothing the way to leave me. I sensed it in her casual touch, in the turns in her life that she did not talk to me about, when her mind drifted off and her eyes clouded.

Her life was moving somewhere else. That much I knew. Her words were not the old words of hers, something odd to me, words that rang hollow and seemed borrowed, as if they came from someone else. "I need space. I need boundaries." These were clichés, so unlike her. She had come to these decisions well before I fully grasped their implications. How serious she was about this, how deadly it all was. She needed to find her way, she kept saying. "I have told you I need time alone."

"Is there someone else?" I blurted out, noticing her reddening face and twisted, angry mouth. "No! Damn you! It is not someone else. That is not the issue. We are."

Often she would just sit in the armchair by the fireplace and cry quietly, her arm clutched against her chest. She knew the hurt she was inflicting on me, and she knew she was hurting herself, too. But she wanted understanding and harmony despite it all. She wanted to save something of us.

It couldn't be that simple.

We had an excess of passion. Everything about us was born out of it: our writing, our nights, our fights, our silences, and fi-

nally her desperate escape from me and the desperate loneliness
that swept me when at last I came to see that I had lost her.

We had our requiems. How many burials could we stand? Those
dirges, talks dissolving into recriminations, revisions of history,
tears. There were no wounds we left untouched. I would find
her collapsed on the sofa, her mind roaming, her face drawn, so
far from me that I no longer could reach across the room. She
would try again and again to explain, to bring reason to what
was intrinsically irrational: "I haven't had a moment to myself,
to find out who I really am, in ten years." I retaliated absurdly,
throwing back at her our early years, when she had needed me
because all she had had before me was that — loneliness.

We had those circular talks for so long that years later I see us
fixed in place, a frozen scene, she on the corner of the sofa and
I listening so intently that I noticed everything about the room
as if it were new, the slanted light from the living room window
casting shadows on the planes of her face, the dents in our Manila furniture, the words of a song she played over and over.

I knew what she wanted. She wanted me to walk out, to put a
blade to it, neatly. But I would not. I had more tormenting ways.
I stayed, carrying my pain for her to see. I had a fantasy, that she
would come to me with that innocence and frailty I had known
and take me by the hand and let me smooth out the folds of her
shirt where it sloped over her shoulders.

I lied like that to myself.

What she said was "I don't love you the way you want me to."

We were having dinner at Louie's Westside Café. I heard her

words in a chamber inside my mind that was all echoes. "I don't love you the way you want me to." I stared at her, suddenly deaf, stunned into silence.

I left for Washington the next day, more interviews to do, and a life to contemplate. Forlorn as one can only be in hotel bars, even in the best hotels, I would leaf through magazines and newspapers, pretending I was not a lonely guest longing for a chair to be pulled up to my side. I would sit the evening through, waiting for the night.

The time had come when almost anything I said irritated her, even on the phone. "I can't talk now. Have to go." She was setting down rules. I no longer had any right to ask about any part of her life, which reduced our conversations to dead air, quick cuts. I would hang up and lie on the bed in my hotel room, smoking, choking back a scream, and by two in the morning I wanted nothing more than to hear her voice. Somehow I would get up the next day.

Friends looked at me with that helpless and pitying expression that people assume when someone is breaking all around them. Tim, now living in Washington, was at a loss, and tried to find a middle point between me and Elizabeth, shaking the ice in his Scotch, fidgeting in the bar's chair. I saw him half a dozen times in Washington and New York, maybe more, during that period.

Once I asked him straight out, "Will she leave me?"

He came at that question with a direct reply rare for him: "Yes," he said. His bulbous eyes bored into mine. Before he could elaborate, his girlfriend joined us, and I knew he couldn't help me out this time.

"You'll get over it," people would say kindly, but it was a refrain that seemed entirely off the point, meaningless to me.

This was not an affair, a chase of mine, fires burning and then a sweep of ashes. And it was not quite a marriage, white dresses and veils and pieces of paper. This was a life, my life. How could I get over a life or the loss of my life? I was insufferable, obsessed, the object of what I so abhorred, pity and sympathy. I think at times I was truly insane.

Toward the end, I would spend days alone in the house, a bottle of wine within reach, cigarette ashes spilling on the rug. I would finally go to bed and stare at the page of a book I was reading, flipping pages regularly, and after an hour I would notice that I hadn't absorbed a single word. I would listen for her footsteps on the stairs, then the click of the bedside lamp in the guest room that she now occupied. For several periods during the last months she was not there at all. She was visiting friends, finding sympathy and consolation, or out of town on stories, finding places and distractions to get away from me.

Those were my worst days, sitting on our sofa all day long, blotting out my life, too dispirited to move, to read, to write. In the late afternoon, when the solitude became intolerable, I would go down to Louie's and pass the time propped up on a barstool, talking with the actor bartender and the comedian waitress, who, being New Yorkers, connoisseurs of the human condition, could easily read the meaning of the lines on my face.

July, and the city was thinning out, people going away for the summer, to the Cape or the Hamptons. It seemed half the town was gone, and I was looking for a place to live, dreary walks up and down Amsterdam and West End Avenue and Riverside, everything I saw square and dark and reeking of lonely nights. I would go out day after day, trying to find something to cheer about but instead finding myself crying in the middle of the street, dreading the aloneness, the finality of it.

I knew I had to move out when she did not come home one night until two in the morning, something she had never done before. I overheard a car slow down, a door open and close, and the key turning in our front door. I waited at the top of the stairs. She looked wretched, from tears perhaps. Her linen jacket was wrinkled as if it had been balled up and thrown, and her eyes were glazed. But she was steady, composed.

"Where have you been?" I demanded. She looked at me as if she had never seen me before. Her facial structure completely changed, her face chiseled foxlike, a gesture of disdain around her mouth. "I don't have to tell you anything," she snapped right back, pulling away from me. I shouted back, followed her into the guest room, groping for words, wanting to wound her. "Get out!" she shouted. Her scream sent a shock wave through me.

I went to my bed and covered myself in a blanket and did not stop shaking until dawn.

That morning I dressed early and left the house to begin looking for an apartment, and for a month I looked in vain for anything I could stand. Giving up, I flew down to Washington. It took me just two days to find an apartment in a stately 1917 building in the Dupont Circle neighborhood. After the awful apartments I had seen in Manhattan, this one was a relief, and Washington itself, serene, clean, and leafy, seemed a safe shelter.

"I have an apartment in Washington," I told her when I returned to New York. I wanted her to be pleased. She staggered. "Oh, God!" She was choked up. "That was fast . . ." Rising from the chair, she came to me and held me.

Our last weeks together had a mournful gentleness. I could see that she was relieved, more affectionate now that our struggle was nearly over. I went through the details of moving, and she agreed easily on the things I could take with me — the New Delhi desk, an old kitchen table, our bed, the black tape deck we had in Manila, the long-armed swayback butaca, my rugs.

On the Sunday before my departure she opened up a magnum of Dom Pérignon, raised her glass to me, and clutched me to her, her arms around my waist, her hair on my face, her breath so light. "You know you cannot chop me out of your life," she said softly, her eyes shining. "If you do, you'll be cursing me and yourself."

She had her music on, and as she held me closely, her chin resting on my head, we moved slowly around the living room, dancing as we never had before — Stay by me and make the moment last . . . Seconds, minutes, an eternity, everything blurred.

She left for her office early that morning, before my movers came. "I don't think I can stand to see you go," she had said the night before. We tried to make the parting quick, couldn't even look at each other or find any words, and when she closed the front door behind her I did not go to the window to watch her walk away. The movers came and went, and I sat on the sofa, ragged but tearless. I moved through the house, the blank spaces where my furniture had been, and it seemed enormous, so silent. Then I walked down to a florist and picked out a couple of brilliant orange Asian tiger lilies and put them in a vase on top of her Chinese chest in the living room. I found an envelope and slipped in it the one thing I wanted to leave her, a yellowing document that my mother had once given me: my first-grade report card, straight A's from geography to arithmetic at the Van Dyke Academy in Mexico City. On the cover of the report card was stapled an oval-shaped photograph of me, a wistful face at the age of five, long, straight dark hair pulled off the forehead with a small bow clasp.

I don't know why I want you to have this, I scribbled on a piece of paper, and sealed the envelope and leaned it against the vase with the tiger lilies.

I picked up my luggage, my duffel, the case with the laptop Elizabeth had given me for one of my birthdays, and my shoulder-strap bag. I found Boom, who was distracted by the birds swooping in the garden, and crushed him in my arms and kissed his head. It was a sunny day, very hot, August third, three weeks short of our seventh year together. I closed the front door and locked it and put my house keys in an envelope and left it for her under the door.

Rush-hour taxis zipped past, and I could hardly lift my hand to hail one, but finally a cab stopped and I lugged the bags onto the back seat and got in.

"LaGuardia," I said, keeping my face turned away from the driver, feeling the tears come slowly, trickling down one by one. Out the window Manhattan rolled by, stranger suddenly than any place I had ever known.

I CAN'T LET GO of that time, can't let it breathe. After all these years I can't find the mystery, and not finding it, I can't tear it out of me. Our last years I can only begin to trace, but even now I can't find the exact location, the damning gesture and the words, the precise moment when the last glass of wine came with passion, and the first came dry, drained of us.

I lie in the mornings wrapped in my old quilt, my hands in fists, a pillow at my back, and I glance out my window, always the first thing I do, and take in the sun that lingers in lilac clouds, the tree limbs slashing at the panes, and the birthday balloon some passerby lost into that tree last summer, now torn, deflated. I noticed today that spring has come, the sun spreads out early, beams across my bed, and there are crocuses and daffodils, sprigs of yellow marigolds, and the blue- and red-chested birds are making nests in brambles beneath the crooked magnolia tree and the drooping wisteria.

I walk the streets every day and every day I stop with a jolt, suddenly seized, at the far sight of an auburn head, the tilt of a neck, the slope of shoulders. I see Elizabeth, hair blowing in her eyes, feathery around her face, combed down her neck, where it arches. She lopes across the street toward me. But she has not seen me, has not seen the stricken face that has to be mine, and I move toward her, wading in air, the moment stilled. Her voice, my name in her voice, rises from the silence I live in, and I lift my face, running to her, and then the voice is gone.

Old songs. Grooves of music, a pounding beat. Adagios and crescendos. Drops of red wine, smoke, the smell of skin freshly soaped, a moist touch of perfume. Must she be, after these years, in everything, in my bloodstream?

In the fall of our first months of separation, I tried to create a world for myself. Washington seemed just right for this, a mostly empty canvas. Washington wasn't Manhattan, Manila, Tokyo, where we had made a trail. Here, the streets bore no reminders, none of our footprints. The faces I saw were unblemished by care, interchangeably bland as I passed by them when I took my morning walk to the newsstand. I was, I knew, invisible, not to them perhaps, but to myself.

Once a day I forced myself to speak, chatting absent-mindedly with the front-desk clerks at my apartment building and with the woman who sold me newspapers and magazines. I tried to hear my voice, to recognize it. How do you like this weather, they asked, rubbing their arms for warmth. There were scraps of frozen snow on the sidewalk, northern skies. "Well, it's winter, isn't it?" I would reply. Later, in the spring and summer, the question changed to "How you like this heat?" I would say, "Well, it's summer, isn't it?" I tried to remember to smile, to give a bright lilt to my greetings while I checked my mailbox in the apartment lobby, knowing it was empty, and walked by a pair of old ladies who always seemed to be seated on the hardwood bench in the foyer, holding their grocery bags, heavy maiden ladies sitting out their mornings, giving me a searching top-to-bottom look, never quite placing me. I passed by them quickly, escaping, and climbed the three flights up the tile staircase to my apartment, only the squeak of my tennis shoes breaking the glum quiet of the hallway.

In the evenings those first months, I walked up the block to a Brazilian grill, a smoky dark-glass storefront, ordered up caipirinhas, and distracted myself by listening to snatches of conversation at the bar, the gossip of waitresses, college girls with huge black-lined eyes, sheened tresses, and tight T-shirts who sidled up to the stool next to mine, wanting to know about my life. I always had a book with me, probably tipping them off that I wasn't the standard bar drinker. It was the orange-spine copy of Graham Greene's *Collected Short Stories* that I had carried on countless trips, thinking I would finish it one day. Over the years I had read only a few pages at a time, in hotels, before dropping off to sleep. I lost track of what I had read but kept my place with a dog-eared yellow Thai Air Lines boarding pass stamped Phuket International Airport and signed in black ink, *Elizabeth, Bangkok 1988.*

Wanting to seem occupied, with a purpose, I clutched the book as if I were too busy for company, content to be left alone, wiping wet rings off the bar counter with my shirtsleeve. I laid the book face-up on the counter and rubbed the cover, the skin of it. I would turn the pages, flipping them like a deck of cards, writing poetic words in my head. It was my way of announcing my presence. I was trying to make a statement, saying that I was really not alone, protecting myself from the solitude that hangs over all lone drinkers.

I did try to see people — you must see people, you must move on, everyone told me. Going to the restaurant, I was trying to set a pace, to unearth myself from entire days where I spoke to no one but shop clerks. I screamed at the world. But the scream was something only I could hear. Friends, acquaintances, came around now and then, a little dinner to perk me up, a double espresso at a coffee bar in the afternoon, but I was absent all the while, not listening, bored, longing. I carried my loss on my face, puffy eyes, lengthening lines around my mouth. Noticing the concerned eyes looking at me, the eyes of people who had suffered their own losses, who had long ago recorded them and closed the books, I felt nothing but a void, no elemental connection, and after two, three hours, I would wander home.

Tim was still living in Washington and would meet me after he got done at work for a drink at the Bombay Club, or at the Ritz-Carlton, and shaking the ice cubes in his gin and tonic, flipping open his pack of Dunhills and tossing it at me, he would exhort, expound, making sense of the world for me. But he seemed impatient. He had moved past me, had left behind the brittle affairs. His heart had grown up, and he no longer needed nights of sour mash whiskey and confessions, his eyes moistening over his adored goddesses. He had passed that stage. He was graying at the temples, thickening around the waist. His life had changed. He had obligations, family duties, his engagement, big wedding plans, two hundred invitations to address, and his work, dealing with national security, breaking stories.

There was something else, too—the discomfort of people in the presence of disaster. He had loved Elizabeth, had brightened up in her presence, the arms she threw around his neck. I had always known that, since that first time at Orchard when he earnestly pleaded with me to leave her alone. Now that she and I had broken up, he was torn, he said. The hurt he saw in each of us was more than he could bear. So for a time he stayed away, worn out by me and the endless grief. He was not the only one to give me a pass. Some old friends disappeared altogether, people whom Elizabeth and I had shared. My messages and letters went unanswered, and for a long time I waited for the phone to ring, for the mail, even when I pretended to myself that I no longer cared.

Slowly I made a routine, a frame I constructed to hold myself in. The apartment I lived in had good light, windows on three sides. I set up my desk and my other things, and it became a refuge, another refuge. I wrote every day and rarely left the building but for excursions down the street just to take into account that there was a world out there. I found myself staring absently into the glass windows of coffee shops, scanning the faces inside, vapid, smug, animated sometimes, engaged in lives of their own. But most of the time I strode by, catching the reflection of sunglasses on a grave face, myself, and I shifted my eyes and moved rapidly past. I could feel no relation to any of it, no fit anywhere.

For months I would not listen to music. I would not open that door. In fits of anger I threw out my Manila notebooks and folders filled with half-done articles and drafts, and I put away a framed picture of her and the rings she had given me. But all that, coming in bursts of crying and remorse, did nothing to take her away. After a time I brought out the picture I had tossed, splitting the wooden frame, on the top of a closet shelf and placed it back just where it had always been. I put back my rings and began to listen to music and sorted through hundreds of loose snapshots of our years together, collecting them in groupings by dates and places, and bound them in rubber bands.

I brought out our letters from the leather bag where I kept them and scattered them on the living room rug. I sat on the rug and opened one, two, then another, and each line, each line of her writing, was a stab. It was then, with her old clipboard and a faded yellow notepad, that I picked up a pen and wrote down a phrase that came from nowhere, and the next day I looked at it and made it into a sentence, and that was the way this story came to me.

She moved to Washington in the late fall, and presently a letter from her came in the mail, a typewritten sheet folded in one of her old crinkly *par avion* envelopes. She had typed it on her Royal, wrote it fast I could see by the crossovers and keys that seemed to run into each other. She had been settling into her new house in Washington, she said lightly, a great house for reading. I pictured it instantly: the sofa, the lamps, and the things that used to be "our" things. She was finding her way in a new place quietly, she said. The letter was light, careful. I looked for words she didn't write, conjured the rhythms of her life. But the truth is that I knew nothing.

"I don't want our lives to crisscross," she had told me a few months earlier, in New York, when she announced that she was

moving to Washington. She had run into me by chance at a restaurant, one of our spots during our years in Manhattan. I was
in from Washington for Halloween weekend, trying to keep in
touch with New York friends and doing some business, when
suddenly there she was in the restaurant, in a rush as usual. She
didn't notice me and went on to sit nearby with a friend, her
back to me. Bracing myself, I got up and walked over and put
my hand on her shoulder. She shuddered and her face turned
pink, a flush broke down her neck, then she recovered, smiled
brightly, and stuck out her hand, cold, clammy, to shake mine.
I knew blood was rushing to my face, my head was pounding,
and I felt sick, but we played on, a casual patter, the lies of false
indifference, and then I went back to my business, watching as
she left the restaurant.

We met by agreement the next day. It was a miserable rainy
afternoon on Times Square. We found a noodle shop, went
through the preambles. Then she said I was to make no effort to
see her once she moved to Washington. She didn't want any of
what she called "our back-and-forth." She looked formidable,
unmovable. I left her in the rain on a sidewalk on Broadway,
tugged at the mustard-colored slicker that made her look like
a 1940s flier. As I leaned forward to embrace her, she stepped
away and barely brushed my neck with her fingers.

Her words rang in my head all the way back to Washington. I
didn't try to find out where in Washington she was moving to, or
when, but I wondered constantly, and one day when I was walking up Connecticut Avenue, near my neighborhood, I stopped at
a real estate office where photos of houses for sale were posted

on the display window. There was an ink sketch of a house with a SOLD banner across it. Somehow I knew it had to be her house; it looked just like her.

I saw her finally. I was going up Connecticut, hunched down in my coat to ward off a brittle winter wind. It was a Saturday, and I had just gone to the store for bread and magazines. I saw her out of the corner of my eye, a flash across the road. I had to look twice. She was running, hair flying, a swatch of lavender sweatshirt and white sweatpants, but by the time I recognized her she had run half a block ahead across the road. I called out to her, shouting, and I ran after her. But I couldn't catch her. I saw her disappear down the road, and I stopped at my street corner, feeling foolish, my body chilled.

The next afternoon I walked across a bridge that spans Rock Creek Park, the bridge she was about to cross when I had lost sight of her. The December wind was blowing hard, unblocked by buildings or trees. The sun was out and people were wearing their sweats, running and biking, swooshing past me. I kept a lookout for her and trudged on against the wind until I came to the end of the bridge. I stopped at the curb, waiting for the light to change, half wishing I hadn't gone out at all.

On that other side of the bridge everyone seemed smug and blond, and toddlers wobbled in hundred-dollar baby running shoes. The suburbs begin just around that point, and on bright shiny weekends the lines form at the ice cream parlor and the restaurants are overrun at brunch. The last thing I wished was to seem forlorn, single. I wanted a destination, a rendezvous. I stopped to read the display menus at the Thai, Indian, and Lebanese restaurants along the strip. I went into a market and bought a pack of cigarettes. I browsed through a gallery of tacky silver crafts and motel art. An hour had gone by and I was leaving a gift shop when I turned my eyes down the street and saw her.

She was walking toward me but had not noticed me. Her neck was wrapped in a long woolen scarf, the collar of her jacket was half turned up; she often forgot to smooth it down. She was swinging a small pink bag from a record store. I stopped dead, watching her, and pushed toward her. I wanted to run but measured each step, and she saw me. She smiled, ah, there you are, and before either of us could say a word, I had thrown my arms around her, feeling the coat, the ridges of her back, her chest, her neck, the ruff of her hair. I had not seen her for three months. Her arms hung limp at her sides but she didn't pull away.

She didn't seem surprised to see me. "I thought I heard your voice shouting my name yesterday when I was running," she said, light in her voice, in her face. "I thought, Well, it's time." She believed in these things, the junctures of history, confluence of moments. "You look great," she said. "But you always looked great in a tan." I had just returned from a spur-of-the-moment four-day trip to Hawaii, a sort of cure I had taken, had read a book lying by a pool in Kauai, spent too much money on bad food, and had too many jet-lagged nights thinking of her and listening to the rustling of palm trees.

We went for coffee and she read a letter I had written her and had carried with me, thinking I would mail it. Her hand was trembling just so, the paper fluttering. "It's beautiful," she said, "as usual." I could not stop staring at her, wanted to take in everything about her. She had on her old blue jeans and a crewneck sweater and a green bandanna rolled around her head.

No lines on her face, no circles under her eyes. Puttering around her yard, getting her house in order, she had slowly burrowed into Washington. We talked for a long time, a few hours, about the changes she saw in me, wounds closing, she said, and she took my hand and held it a second, and then it was dusk and we picked up our coats and walked toward the street where she lived, and at the corner where she had to turn, we stopped. I lit a cigarette, scrubbed the ashes on the sidewalk, unable to pull away. Then she said, "Would you like to come over for a glass of wine, maybe on Christmas?"

I wore a silk blouse and jeans and black flats and my dark jacket and fluffed my hair and practiced a carefree smile. On Christmas morning I took a cab to her house, which was the house that I had picked out as hers from the sketch at the real estate office. She watched me get out of the car and walk up the brick steps to her doorway. "It's strange," she said, "to see you arriving by taxi." I knew what she meant—arriving as a guest, a stranger.

She had built a fire. Boom was curled down on the back cushion of an armchair, and the Christmas tree was trimmed with the things we had collected since Manila. The furniture that had been ours was placed against Navajo-white walls; the old wooden sculpture of a lion's head from India was hung above the mantelpiece; the rugs I knew so well were scattered in all the rooms of her house, in the living room, in the bedrooms upstairs. She showed me around, a little nervous, and I climbed the staircase behind her and went into every room and did not touch anything, the house so definitely hers.

She went into the kitchen, sun-white, red-tiled, and brought out a silver platter on which she had arranged slices of smoked salmon and a cream cheese and caviar dip she made for big occasions, and we sat on the rug in the living room. She had put effort into all of this, wanted it to go smoothly, a perfect reunion. All the afternoon through we talked as we always could all those years, about writing and books, and my magazine assignments with *Vanity Fair,* but we did not talk about us, and she touched my hand and threw more logs on the fire and shifted the ashes and brought out more wine and I lit her cigarettes.

Her knees brushed mine, we were seated that close, and the flames off the fire made her face glow as if she were newly in love. I had a sense of time not having moved at all, of things in their proper place, and the loneliness eased off. But I knew anything could change this, that we were testing each other, calibrating words, checking the drift of the conversation. There was nothing neutral; there was nothing that was not fraught. I knew I could not cross that wall of privacy she put up around her to keep me out. But with her I couldn't maintain distance for any length of time. Three glasses of wine, and I was reckless. I began to probe and poke into our relationship, what had gone wrong, and what her new life was like without me — the things she did not want to talk about. She immediately shut down, folding herself. Rising off the floor, she moved to the farthest armchair, put her knees up defensively against her chest, and tucked her hands in her armpits. I persisted, pushing her, and spilled wine on the rug. I mumbled apologies, mortified. I had ruined the day.

She drove me home in anger and silence. Halfway to my place I blurted out, "How do you feel about me?"

I glanced over at her. She was looking straight ahead, and after taking a long moment to phrase her reply, she said, "If you mean, do I love you like I used to? No." I said nothing; I was numbed. We arrived at my building and I thanked her, got out of her car, and closed the door carefully. I didn't want to slam it. I didn't want to run into the building. I wanted to walk away very slowly.

"Worst winter we've had around here," the old ladies in my building said day after day, in January and February and March, the winter of 1994. The doorman worried about me: "Girl, how you going out there without gloves and scarf?" Seasons caught me by surprise. I always had too many layers or not enough, maybe because I had grown up in the tropics where seasons don't change, maybe because it seemed silly to me to carry rubber boots and umbrellas in the rain, and earmuffs in the snow.

But, God, I froze that winter, shivered through days and nights in my apartment, the wind sifting through the cracks around the air conditioners. That winter gave me an understanding of the rhythms one creates to keep life within. I learned to live alone. Cork walls around me, silence. Vast, empty nights. I would lie on the sofa, listening to Brahms, or maybe Schubert, Annie Lennox, or the Manila Blues tapes, watching the amber lights of the building across the street, the men in undershirts moving behind half-drawn blinds, and in the mornings the garbage trucks came and the buses coughed and cranked, and the world came to my door, and I knew that another day stretched before me, without voices, without someone for dinner, without the phone call I always waited for.

Months passed. One night quite late the phone broke the si-

lence, Elizabeth on the line, and when I heard her voice, everything about her came back to me, the way she said my name, the
solitude that was in her and had been mine. She was muttering,
crying, but I couldn't make out what she was saying. I wanted to
keep her on the phone, but she hung up and I was left in the dark
of my apartment.

Much later, one Sunday morning, she appeared at my door. I
was still in my robe, hair springing in unruly curls. She looked
exactly the way she looked that first day we spent together in
Manila, in March 1986: panting, sweating, red-faced from a two-
mile run from her house, in madras shorts, her chest damp in an
old familiar T-shirt. "I've been wanting to see the place you live
in," she said. "Saw you the other day when I drove by—you
were looking out the window." She took in the apartment in a
couple of strides, liked it, said it reminded her of Manila. She
took up a corner of the sofa, taking my coffee, while I fumbled
with cigarettes, smiling helplessly. She fit in perfectly in the
apartment, and I realized for the first time that I had made the
place for her, that every bookshelf, every rug, every piece of
furniture, had something of hers.

"You live like a writer," she said approvingly. She would say
this frequently, as a compliment, that it was the life she wanted.
She made a romance of this life, and so much of it was true, and
we talked about that, and over the next months she invited me
to dinner at her house, and we would call each other up like we
used to, for no reason at all, just to check in, and we drank wine
and at times it seemed to me that there was no space between us.

On the day of Tim's wedding in May, we stood side by side
among people we had known since our first year. Seated next

to me, while poetry was read and songs played, she clasped her hands, my rings still there. I could hardly breathe and played with the rings she had given me, daydreaming. We filed out of the church together, and with every step I felt her arm brushing against me. Later, we toasted each other with sparkling wine and drifted in and out of the wedding party and circled back to each other, like an old married couple, she said, teasing. When she was set to leave, I walked her out and she draped an arm around me, pulling me to her. "We have such cinematic moments," she said, laughing, and then she picked up her bag and walked off. I thought she was crying.

I left the apartment building that summer, just around the time a couple moved next door with a snake. The old ladies, who learned about the snake too late to stop it, were beside themselves. "That snake has to go," they shouted at the concierge, who rolled her eyes, commiserating and patting their backs. The snake was the most exciting thing that happened in the building in the year I lived there.

It seemed that I moved every August—to Manila, to New York, from New York to Washington. Now I was moving again. This time it was a short move, from Dupont Circle to Georgetown. I rented a two-story brick house with a patio out back and a magnolia tree, bamboo stands, and azaleas in bloom. Elizabeth came over to look it over, snooped around it, ran up the stairs, opened closet doors, and helped me pick out the right shade of white for the walls. No buildings hovered over this place. A tree out front on the sidewalk was all you could see from the living room, and the eastern light flooded the place through white shutters. "You could make love in here and no one would see you," she said, and I wondered.

But for periods of time, without explanation, she would remove herself from my life. Sometimes we talked for six hours straight, and sometimes not for months. Twisting on a string, I was always reading between her words, setting them in ink, recording them, analyzing, interpreting, snaring myself. She used to say that I knew no limits, that given a drop of water I wanted the entire Pacific, that she had to keep me far from her, and we fought about this. She drew the lines I constantly crossed. She would then try to set the terms of our separation and build a fence around herself, excluding me. "I am so sick that I cannot express it, going back and forth, continuing this fight," she said over and over, wanting me to stay away, but I didn't quite believe it.

She had a way of capturing me always, with a line of writing, with a look, the morning she brought me marigolds from her garden, the afternoon in her house when she came up behind me and held me briefly in her arms, the day when she cried as she told me, "I've never been able to walk away from what we have been." There were the letters she wrote me from another one of her bloody islands, the oil painting of a young girl that she brought me back from Haiti, and the vintage rum and coconut liqueur, as if she were bringing back pieces of my roots in the Caribbean. She always wanted to take me back to my childhood, the flavor and smell of those tropical places, the cacophony of street people talking all at once, the brilliant palette of dreams born and shattered.

There are days now when I imagine her in those places, running down a rutted road, sweat pouring down her smudged face. There are hours, long hours, when I hear her music, the music she played in that room at the Manila Hotel, and I can feel the floor shaking under her feet, her head swinging around, a cigarette dangling off a corner of her mouth, a margarita in her hand, arms floating, flaying, and her voice rising high, as if no one could hear her, singing out,

Take me to the river
drop me in the water . . .

In all this time I have learned to live without her. I have learned to be alone. That is different from learning to live alone. I don't mean living alone with an office to go to where you can hear voices, have a drink after work, and I don't mean having family and friends close by, on the telephone, in the next town, dropping in. I mean alone, weeks spent in entire solitude, locked in, mute to the world, days and weeks when picking up the mail that comes through the front-door chute may be an occasion, hoping each day for the slant of a familiar handwriting, days when you walk by the telephone hoping it will ring, and when it doesn't, you want to shout, *Is anyone out there?*

It is the life she had imagined for me, a life without soirees and salons, without frippery, distractions, or intrusions. I have become what I believe she saw in me, what I had dreamed for myself. There are days when the early-morning sun comes through the windows and falls on this desk and the air has the tinge of summer in it and I play my music, strings and violins, and the old Manila tapes, and I dance alone with a freedom I didn't have then, not even then.

Sometimes I believe that ours was a love that lived outside us, that it had its own force that had nothing to do with our will, with promises made and moods and fear. I imagine it as an unbroken circle, widening and narrowing but always holding us within it.

We want to discard what we no longer need. Not only do we want to dispose of it, but we want to obliterate it, to kill our onetime need of it. But we want to believe too that the totems we trusted had magic, a kind of protection against evil—the absence of passion—can save us.

We vest in our love a kind of sanctity. We frame it and hang it on our walls, we arrange it so around us, like icons and saints. The lamp she gave me, the black typewriter, the pictures of another time and another place, this desk. These are only objects in the end, possessing nothing but the curves and planes, the visible, palpable symbols of what we were to each other. Now they sit inert, without magic or power, detached from what we have become.

I have not put them away in a basement. I don't want them out of sight; I don't want them taken from me. But they are no longer the crucibles of those years. I have stopped kneeling at those stations of the cross. I knelt for so long.

How little we know about passion. How wretched it is. How imperfect. We don't understand the transfiguration it brings, the delusion, and we shudder at its harrowing pain. I have looked at it for so long, its flowering and its decay, but I don't know it truly, cannot yet find the place where it comes from, and yet I know that there is no life without it. Terror is its companion, and loneliness, and desolation, abandonment, perhaps, in the end. We are all fractured, broken somewhere, and passion, this passion of ours, that moment when for once we feel at one with the other, is the only refuge, the only peace we can know.

I have no choices now, in this blanched city where Sundays fall into an easy stupor, where benign churches, redolent with lilies, fill with people who never raise their voices. I want the milky green of plants in the tropics, the loud voices that rent the air, the dust in my face. Her fingers in my hair.

The sky here, and all the spring skies of this place of robins and cardinals, her kind of place, this sky over me has no traces today of clouds. It is perfect, cerulean, azure, azul, all the words we use to describe a sky that is simply itself, pristine, newborn. You want to reach up and hold it in your arms.

I close my eyes and I am listening to her voice. I lay my head back on the sofa, my hair falling over my ears, spilling on the back of the cushion. I feel her moving, coming closer, her fingers barely touching my chin, lifting my face, her breath on my skin. Her face is now on mine, a light, infinite.

Acknowledgments

I owe Kathy Robbins just about everything. A brilliant agent, gifted editor, and a consummate ally, Kathy has been my anchor for nearly two decades. In all that time, she has been fiercely loyal, demanding, and generous. Her team at the Robbins Office — David Halpern, Louise Quayle, Mike Gillespie, Rachelle Bergstein, and Arielle Asher — is an indispensable support system, always smart, thoughtful, and gracious.

My editors at Houghton Mifflin Harcourt took to this book with enthusiasm and heart. George Hodgman, who acquired the book, gave it his keen eye and sensibility, and Andrea Schulz and Christina Morgan contributed their exceptional talents and skills. Thanks are hardly enough for everyone else who worked on the book at HMH, including Alison Kerr Miller for her terrific copyediting; Lisa Glover for orchestrating production; Patrick Barry for the book jacket and Melissa Lotfy for the interior design; Christina Mamangakis and Ayesha Mirza for introducing the book to the world; Loren Isenberg for expert advice; and Johnathan Wilber for keeping me on my toes.

My deepest gratitude to my family: my sister Angeles, now gone, remains a constant inspiration; my sisters Carmen, Sara, and Olga stayed by me through difficult stretches, always encouraging even when there was little to encourage; my brothers, Amaury and Hank, along with my magnificent nieces and nephews, cheered me on from the sidelines.

I owe a lifelong debt of gratitude to colleagues and friends in Manila for their invaluable friendship and camaraderie over the years I lived there. To all of them, *salamat po!*

A number of wonderful editors and writers have offered advice, support, and friendship along the way, especially Alison Smale, Elise O'Shaughnessy, Carolyn Lee, Gloria Anderson, Gene Roberts, Joe Lelyveld, Susan Kamil, Robin Desser, Tina Brown, Graydon Carter, Klara Glowczewska, Reinaldo Herrera, Michael Caruso, Jennifer Hershey, Seth Mydans, Jim Naughton, Danielle Mattoon, and Jill Abramson.

For a variety of reasons, I owe much more than I could ever say to Tim, Andy, Mirta Ojito, Mark Bulik, Mark Fineman, Jennifer Mlekoday, Adam Platt, Tif Loehnis, Tom Christie, Kate Doyle, Nan Doyle, Susanna Doyle, Victoria Doyle, Kate Platt, Greg Brock, Jane Ashley, Mari Mater O'Neill, Liane Ramírez, Monica Corcoran, Amy Blackstone, Julia Preston, Trudy Rubin, Fran Dauth, Jennifer Preston, Belén Fidalgo, and Margaret Scott.

LLT
New York, New York
August 31, 2011